THINKING CRITICALLY ABOUT RESEARCH

We live in an age of unprecedented access to information. The last decade has seen an exponential growth in data and material available, often at the touch of a button. However, this has also made it harder to discern between fact and fiction. What is real and what is fake? What should we believe and what should we reject?

In an environment of information overload, a distrust of experts, the circulation of misinformation and false facts, and public debates based upon poor evidence, *Thinking Critically About Research* comes at a vital time. The book is designed to help readers develop a critical understanding of evidence and the ways in which evidence is presented, and to challenge the information they receive in both academic and non-academic sources. The author presents a step-by-step approach with a focus on knowing methods, thinking critically about methods and thinking critically about presentation which culminates in a bespoke 'critical tool kit' which offers a practical checklist designed to be used when reading, interpreting, or carrying out research.

Also containing learning features including tasks and worked examples, drawing on real research studies, this is an essential resource for students and researchers, for those putting research into practice, and for those communicating research to others who want to have better critical thinking skills.

Jane Ogden is a Professor in Health Psychology at the University of Surrey where she teaches psychology, nutrition, dietician, vet, and medical students to think critically about research. She has published over 190 papers and eight books.

THINKING CRITICALLY ABOUT RESEARCH

A STEP-BY-STEP APPROACH

JANE OGDEN

Routledge
Taylor & Francis Group

LONDON AND NEW YORK

First published 2019
by Routledge
2 Park Square, Milton Park, Abingdon, Oxon OX14 4RN

and by Routledge
711 Third Avenue, New York, NY 10017

Routledge is an imprint of the Taylor & Francis Group, an informa business

British Library Cataloguing-in-Publication Data
A catalogue record for this book is available from the British Library

Library of Congress Cataloging-in-Publication Data
A catalog record for this book has been requested

ISBN: 978-0-367-00019-6 (hbk)
ISBN: 978-0-367-00020-2 (pbk)
ISBN: 978-0-429-44496-8 (ebk)

Typeset in Bembo
by Apex CoVantage, LLC

MIX
Paper from
responsible sources
FSC
www.fsc.org   FSC® C013056

Printed and bound in Great Britain by
TJ International Ltd, Padstow, Cornwall

CONTENTS

CONTENTS

ACKNOWLEDGEMENTS

This book is a product of years of teaching and getting feedback from my students about what does and doesn't work. I am therefore grateful to every student who has sat in my seminars or lectures particularly if they have given me eye contact, smiled at me when I am going on about something, put their hand up to answer a question, shared their anecdotes, and even occasionally laughed at my jokes. I am also grateful to all the students I have supervised over the years who have helped me refine my attempts at explanation, used my scribbled diagrams, and asked the right questions. My thanks also go to Ash O'Keeffe for reading an earlier draft for me with her undergraduate eye.

I am also grateful to Russell George from Taylor and Francis for supporting me with this book and helping me think through how it might work best.

Finally, my thanks also go to my children Harry and Ellie who are just wonderful and make me proud every day and to David Armstrong for still wanting to have conversations about methodology, truth, and science even after 23 years.

OVERVIEW

I have taught for 30 years, but have got much more pleasure from encouraging students to question the notion of truth than just teaching them facts. I have written many straightforward academic papers and books but have found it far more exciting to question science than to practice it and in my heart I was very much a relativist who mocked those naïve enough to still believe in evidence and truth. But then 2016 happened. Brexit and Trump revealed my need to be able to shout 'liar', 'false', 'wrong', and 'surely you can't believe that'? at the TV, all of which exposed my hidden faith in reality. And family and friends' health issues saw me resort to the need for evidence based practice as I became frustrated with one friend's determination to follow a fad diet, another's unnecessary and probably dangerous mammograms, and a doctor's determination to put my father on statins. It seems that deep down I am less of a relativist than I thought. And what I have realised is that it is good to question truth, fact, and evidence. But that this must be done from an informed position of understanding how evidence is generated in the first place. And what I have also realised is that in this post-truth world when people are flooded with information, they have become deskilled in knowing how to separate this information into fact and fiction, truth and myth, and evidence that is worth the paper it is written on, and evidence that is not. And once they have these critical thinking skills, then, and only then, can they play with relativism, but not before.

ABOUT THIS BOOK

Over the past 30 years, an explosion of information has created information overload, a distrust of experts, the circulation of misinformation and false facts, and public debates based upon poor evidence. This has been called the 'post-truth world' and I think there are two possible solutions to this problem. The first is to accept that 'anything goes' and embrace a post-modern world in which all information is deemed equal. The second is to stay critical and develop a critical understanding of evidence and the ways in which this evidence is presented. This book will first describe the need for being critical generated by information overload. It will then offer a solution in terms of being critical of both what evidence there is and how it is presented. This will culminate in the critical tool kit, which focuses on methods, measurement, analysis, theory, and the power of persuasion. Lecturers are forever telling their students to be more critical but students rarely understand what this means. This book should be essential reading for all students who want to know what being critical means and for lecturers who want their students to be more critical. It is also relevant to anyone wishing to become skilled in the art of critical thinking for their daily lives.

ABOUT THE AUTHOR

I am a Professor in Health Psychology at the University of Surrey where I teach health psychology, research methods, and critical thinking to psychology, medical, vet, and nutrition students. I also carry out my own research using a wide range of methods on a number of different topics. I am author of five academic books and three trade books and 190 academic papers. I am also a regular contributor to the media through TV, radio, newspapers, and magazines and am passionate about communicating science in a way that is useful and relevant.

••

WHO IS THIS BOOK FOR?

People in all walks of life need to understand research. Whether we are students, health professionals, teachers, lecturers, journalists, or broadcasters or even just as parents or people, research forms the basis of every decision we make, everything we do, and everything we believe to be right. We therefore need to be able to critically evaluate the strength of any research we read or hear about and assess whether it is credible, weak, or just plain wrong. This book aims to show people in a step-by-step way how to think critically about research. It can be used by different people in different ways.

> **As a module:** This book could be used as a module to teach students what we mean by being critical. It consists of 11 chapters that take the reader through the stages of knowing research methods (the basics, design, measurement, data analysis). It then shows how to think critically about research in terms of what evidence there is (the basics, design, measurement, data analysis, theory), and how this evidence is presented (strategies of persuasion). It culminates in the critical tool kit that is a useful (and simple) checklist of key critical thinking terms and shows how critical thinking can be used in our day-to-day lives. Then for those who want to be extra critical it unpacks the notion of

scientific truth, explores the fundamental assumptions of any given discipline, and explores the role of critical thinking in a broader sense in terms of thinking outside of the box. It consists of several learning features such as tasks to be completed and worked examples and draws upon real research studies from all walks of life which could be used as the basis of lectures, class discussions, or homework.

> **A module for whom?** Students of psychology, sociology, social science, medicine, dentistry, veterinary medicine and those allied to medicine such as nurses, occupational therapists, physiotherapists all use research and all need to be more critical. It could also be used by those deciding to carry out research as part of their work such as those in marketing, PR, and project managers.

For upskilling: Research is the basis for clinical practice, education, and scientific writing and reporting. Yet many people using research in their working lives have never been taught what it means and how to evaluate it. This book could be used by anyone who needs to use research as means to upskill and become a better critical thinker.

> **Who needs upskilling?** Anyone who translates research into practice (e.g. doctors, nurses, paramedics, occupational therapists, physiotherapists, counsellors, psychologists, teachers) or anyone who disseminates research to others (journalists, broadcasters, and even bloggers).

For life: Critical thinking is also central to everyday life. Each decision we make is in some way evidence based and we need to evaluate this evidence in order to make sure our decisions are the best they can be. Whether we are deciding what to eat, how to stay well, whether to go to the doctor, what school to send our children to, and even what car to buy we need some understanding of the research out there and some assessment of what we should believe and what we should ignore.

> **Who?** We live in a world of information overload and yet we need this information in order to live our lives both at work and home. Everyone therefore needs to be better at critical thinking so they can sort out the myths from the facts, the lies from the truths, and decide whether whatever evidence they read is strong, weak, or just wrong.

FEATURES OF THIS BOOK

This book describes how to think critically about research in terms of what evidence there is. It also describes how to critically analyse how evidence is being presented and how all sorts of writing is designed to persuade us to believe what is written. To do this the book is full of features to bring the ideas alive. It has tasks to complete to test your understanding; worked examples to show how the ideas presented can be put into practice with specific research studies; figures to illustrate some of the key problems with research; a simple critical tool kit of key critical thinking terms; and a list of further reading for those who want to delve more deeply. I have taught methods and critical thinking in various guises to all sorts of people over the years. I hope the features of this book and the way it is structured illustrates not only that critical thinking is important but also what it actually means to do it. Good luck!

1   WHY DO WE NEED TO BE CRITICAL?

● ●

OVERVIEW

Over the past 30 years, there has been a proliferation of information through an increase in published research, access to the internet, and the explosion of social media. We also gather our information from a vast array of sources including films, the radio, magazines, friends, and colleagues. This chapter will explore the problem of information overload and why we need to develop skills to think critically about research. It then describes what it is reasonable to expect from research and outlines the step-by-step approach for thinking critically about research used in this book.

● ●

INFORMATION OVERLOAD

The first academic journal called Philosophical Transactions of the Royal Society was published in 1665. Between then and 2010 it is estimated that about 50 million papers have been published (Jinha, 2010). Further, in 2006 Björk, Annikki, and Lauri estimated that 1.346 million articles were published in 23,750 journals and in 2009 it was estimated that there were about 25,400 peer-reviewed journals publishing about 1.5 million articles a year. These numbers are still increasing at about 2.5% per year (The National Science Board) although this may have increased even further within the past few years since the Open Access drive and the explosion of online journals. Currently, PubMed, the online data base for medically related research contains 19 million papers, whereas Scopus and the ISI Web of Knowledge which also include the humanities have about 40 million papers. There has also been a parallel growth in the number of researchers of about 3% per year with there now being about 5–10 million researchers depending on the definition used. Of these about 20% publish more than one paper (Jinha, 2010). That is a lot of research to read.

Our information, however, also comes from a range of other sources. In 2017, the ONS reported that 90% of households in Great Britain have internet access, which has increased from only 57% in 2006. Of these, 73% access the internet on their phone 'on the go' which is twice the rate of 36% in 2011.

1

Across the world, the percentage of the population that uses the internet is as follows: Africa 35.2%; Asia 48.1%; Europe 85.2%; Latin America/Caribbean 67%; Middle East 64.5%; North America 95%; Oceania/Australia 68.9%. The world total is 54.5%. The ONS survey in Great Britain also showed that the largest rise between 2007 and 2014 was for using the internet to read or download newspapers or magazines (from 20% to 55%).

Social media is now also a common source of information. Twitter was set up in 2006 when the first tweet was sent by its creator Jack Dorsey. By 2007, there were on average 5,000 tweets per day and it took 3 years until 2009 to reach the billionth tweet. Now there are about 500 million tweets per day and about 200 billion per year, which works out as 350,000 per minute. Similarly, Facebook currently has 1,754,000,000 monthly active users, which has increased by 13.2% between 2014 and 2016. These users spend an average of 18 minutes per Facebook visit and 48% log in on any given day.

Yet, we don't just get information from research articles, the internet, or social media. Whenever we watch a film, turn on the TV, listen to the radio, read a newspaper or magazine, or speak to a friend, nuggets

Task 1 Where do you get your information from?

Have a look at the words below and think where your information comes from on a daily basis. What facts have you recently learned about and where from?

of information come our way. I have learned all about shark attacks from watching 'Jaws' and a lot about how pirates have guidelines not rules from 'The Pirates of the Caribbean'. I also feel pretty qualified as an emergency doctor from watching '24 hours in A and E' on the TV and 'Call the Midwife' has definitely taught me about medicine in London in the 1960s. Task 1 illustrates where I get my information. Have a look at Task 1 and think where you get yours.

• •

THE PROBLEM

This process of information overload is fantastic in many ways as the days of standing in musty libraries, queuing at the photocopier, or starring at a microfiche are over (if you know what these are). It is so much easier to find information on anything that you want simply with a quick search and a press of the mouse. However, it also means that there is just too much information and with this comes the problem of deciding what to believe and what to dismiss. At times, this problem might simply be a problem of source. It is therefore easier to reject information that looks like Task 3 and appears in sources that feel less credible.

It may also be easier to accept information that looks like Task 2 as these are academic journals which appear far more convincing.

Task 2 The role of source: do these sources make information seem more credible?

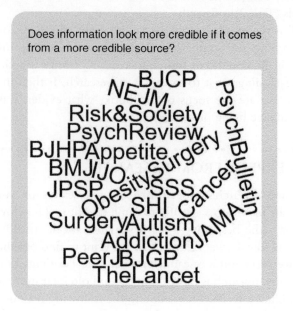

Task 3 The role of source: do these sources make information look less credible?

Does information seem less credible when it comes from less credible sources? Is this a reasonable place to start critical thinking?

TheStandard
FHM
PrivateEye
Twitter
TheDailyMail Metro
FinancialTimes
Psychologies
TheIndependent
Time
Wikipedia
Telegraph
Hello
Men'sHealth
HeraldTribune
WashingtonPost
Playboy
Cosmopolitan
NewYorker
Vogue

But source is by no means the best way to sort information into the accept and reject piles as it is quite likely that the information in less credible sources (Task 3) contains elements of truth whereas the information in academic journals (Task 2) is flawed.

The skill is therefore to think critically about all information, not only taking into account the source but also the content of the information as well as how it is presented. For thinking critically about research, this process involves understanding what to expect from research. It then involves asking two questions that are the focus of this book 'what evidence is there'? and 'how is the evidence being presented'?

WHAT TO EXPECT FROM RESEARCH

From the outside, research can seem like a simple search for truth with each study offering an answer to a specific research question. Therefore, if we want to know 'what is the best way to teach students' we do a study, analyse the results, and know the answer. Likewise, if we want to find out the best way to treat cancer, we carry out a research study and treat patients in line with the findings. In reality, research is more complex and often far more disappointing than we would like it to be. This is due to the following reasons:

Research is always flawed: As this book will show, all studies are flawed in some way whether it be due to their sample, design, measures, or analysis. All research findings need to be understood in the context of these flaws.

The role of uncertainty: All research involves an element of risk, probability, and uncertainty. Consequently, the results from most studies are never true for all of the people all of the time, but only true for some of the people some of the time. This is manageable within the academic world when researchers can acknowledge this uncertainty and incorporate it into their next research study. It becomes more problematic when trying to communicate the findings to a lay audience who want a more definite answer than 'it depends'. It is also a problem when translating research into practice whether it be to inform education, health care, or even the law. We might know that an intervention works better than usual practice, but we can never know whether it works for this one person standing in front of us.

Real–life limitations: There are many real-life limitations which impact upon what research can be done. These may be financial limitations that can reduce the sample size, limit the accessibility to equipment, influence the choice of measurement tools (cheap self-report measures rather than expensive blood tests or scans), or reduce the number of collaborators and the geographical reach of a study. It might also be time limitations with researchers having busy jobs and only being able to do so much. These real-life factors can also limit the level of follow up for any study, as most funding bodies rarely fund studies with follow ups for more than one (sometimes two) years and researchers may not want to devote more than a few years on a single study (when a 30 year follow up would be ideal for the research question).

Ethical considerations: Research is also limited by ethical considerations. The perfect design might be to randomly allocate half the sample to smoke 20 cigarettes per day for 30 years and then see who dies. This isn't ethical. It might also be to pump out carbon dioxide into the atmosphere for 50 years and see if the climate changes. Again – not ethical.

What is feasible: Feasibility also limits research. We might want people to eat a low fat diet for 40 years to see if this prevents heart disease. But people will not stick to it and it's just not feasible to ask them to do this. We also might want half the world to run 5 km every weekend for 20 years to see if they develop stronger bones than the other half of the world, but again this isn't going to happen. Feasibility is a huge block for the ideal research study.

We may have high expectations from research but in reality, all research is flawed and limited by cost, time, ethics, and what is feasible. It is therefore key to accept

5

that research may not be perfect but it can be good enough. This doesn't mean that research should be accepted without criticism. Thinking critically about research involves acknowledging that no research is perfect, then critically analysing why it isn't perfect and what the implications of these imperfections are for any conclusions made. This book shows how this can be done.

THINKING CRITICALLY ABOUT RESEARCH: A STEP-BY-STEP GUIDE

This book offers a step-by-step guide to thinking critically about research and asks two questions 'what evidence is there'? and 'how is the evidence presented'? The steps are as follows:

STEP 1: KNOWING METHODS

Before you can critically analyse research you need to know your methods. This first step offers a clear understanding of the basics of research including research questions, variables and the sample, describes the different types of research designs and their strengths and weaknesses, illustrates the different approaches to measurement, and covers qualitative and quantitative data analysis.

STEP 2: THINKING CRITICALLY ABOUT WHAT EVIDENCE THERE IS

Once you know your methods, the next step is to think critically about all the stages involved in research including sampling, design, measurement, data analysis, and theory. This can be done through being aware of a wide range of issues such as researcher and responder bias, reverse causality and the third factor problem, poor operationalisation of measures, and a recognition of the assumptions underlying data analysis and theory.

STEP 3: THINKING CRITICALLY ABOUT HOW EVIDENCE IS PRESENTED

Research is presented in research articles in respected journals and through a wide range of different media outlets. However, regardless of where it is presented, this process of dissemination always involves a number of persuasive strategies to convince the reader of the credibility of the work. This third step describes these different persuasive strategies and shows how they are apparent in all sorts of writing and impact upon what we believe to be true and what we reject.

STEP 4: USING THE CRITICAL TOOL KIT

This fourth step involves pulling together all the key ideas and terms from the previous three steps into one Critical Tool Kit that can be used to think critically about research whether presented as a research paper in an academic journal, downloaded from the internet, seen on social media, or read from the newspaper as you are eating your fish and chips. It also covers how to use critical thinking in everyday life in terms of dealing with facts, making logical decisions, and dealing with uncertainty.

STEP 5: BEING EXTRA CRITICAL

The previous four steps are sufficient to become a good critical thinker as they cover the questions 'what evidence is there'? and 'how is it presented'? This final chapter explores how to take thinking critically about research to a higher level in terms of notions of truth, the assumptions inherent in any discipline, and thinking outside of the box.

IN SUMMARY

Together with all the films we watch, newspapers we read, and conversations we have, the proliferation of research papers, the development of the internet, and the use of social media has resulted in information overload. This problem creates the need to be able to think critically so we can decide what to believe and what to reject. In terms of research, thinking critically involves accepting that research can only be good enough as it is always flawed in some way and limited by cost, time, feasibility, or ethics. However, thinking critically also involves understanding why and how research is flawed and how this affects any conclusions that can be made. It is also a core life skill. This is the focus of this book.

STEP 4: USING THE CRITICAL TOOL KIT

STEP 5: BEING EXTRA CRITICAL

STEP 1
KNOWING METHODS

2   KNOWING THE BASICS

● ●

OVERVIEW

Whether it is laboratory research using test tubes and drugs, observational research about different tribes in South America, questionnaire research to assess people's beliefs, or a clinical trial to evaluate which intervention works best; all research has some basic features in common. Thinking critically about research requires an understanding of these basic features. This chapter describes these basic features of research focusing on identifying a research area, the types of research questions and variables used, the sample, and the overall story.

● ●

THE BASIC FEATURES OF RESEARCH

All research involves an attempt to understand what is happening in the world. In addition, all research involves the same basic features shown in Figure 1. These are the focus of this chapter.

● ●

IDENTIFYING A RESEARCH AREA

Research is an accumulative process with each new research study building upon the existing literature. It is therefore extremely rare for any one study to change the way that people think or behave and most knowledge develops in a slow and incremental way. Before embarking upon a research study, researchers therefore need to know the existing research to find the gap to fill with their new study. Some researchers also locate their research within theory.

> **Knowing existing research.** Due to the existence of online search engines and data bases of research studies it has become much easier to search the literature than the days of dusty libraries and photocopies (or even microfiches). However, this technological advance has also led to an explosion of research studies meaning that there is now much more to search. Researchers therefore need to search the existing research and

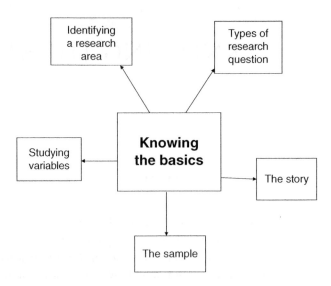

Figure 1 Knowing the basics.

review the evidence. Alternatively, they can find reviews that have already been carried out. There are two key types of literature review: **narrative reviews** are broad and useful for setting the scene for any given area but don't have search strategies that can be replicated by others. A narrative review may ask the question 'How can obesity be treated'? **Systematic reviews** are narrow and focused with specific search terms and search engines. A systematic review would ask 'What factors predict weight loss after dieting for obesity'? Both types of review can be informed by **meta-analyses**, which are a way to synthesise very similar research studies to find an answer to a clear research question. A meta-analysis would ask 'how much weight do people lose after dieting for obesity'? A critical evaluation of a systematic review and meta-analysis is shown in Worked Example 1.

Building or testing a theory. Some researchers also locate their research within a theoretical framework and build either upon this framework or test a specific aspect of a theory. Theories are sometimes also referred to as 'laws', 'models', 'frameworks', or 'approaches' and there is a detailed literature on what does or does not constitute a theory and whether a theory should be testable (and therefore falsifiable). Some theories are broad based such as evolutionary theory, chaos theory, or psychosomatic theory and some are more focused and specific such as 'Newton's laws', 'The Theory of Planned Behaviour', or even 'Gravity'. Theories are used to frame research to contribute to the incremental process of building knowledge within a specific literature. Theories are also used to generate specific hypotheses that can then be tested. Some disciplines

Worked Example 1 A systematic review (SR) and meta-analysis (MA).

Stress and wound healing (Walburn, Vedhara, Hankins, Rixon, & Weinman, 2009)

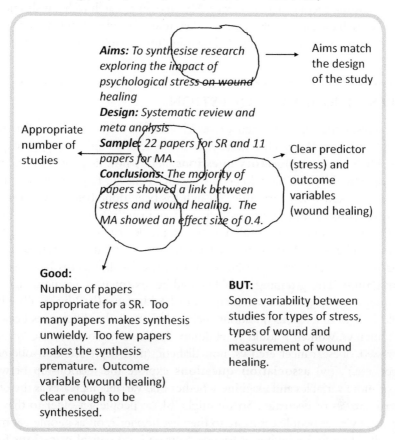

Aims: To synthesise research exploring the impact of psychological stress on wound healing

→ Aims match the design of the study

Design: Systematic review and meta analysis

Appropriate number of studies ←

Sample: 22 papers for SR and 11 papers for MA.

Conclusions: The majority of papers showed a link between stress and wound healing. The MA showed an effect size of 0.4.

→ Clear predictor (stress) and outcome variables (wound healing)

Good:
Number of papers appropriate for a SR. Too many papers makes synthesis unwieldy. Too few papers makes the synthesis premature. Outcome variable (wound healing) clear enough to be synthesised.

BUT:
Some variability between studies for types of stress, types of wound and measurement of wound healing.

are more theory bound than others. In the social sciences, there is a drive to frame all research with theory and to use theory to justify whatever research questions are asked. In contrast, other disciplines such as medicine and health services research are more concerned with whether something works rather than what theory it comes from.

Finding the gap. In some disciplines there remains the tradition of replication whereby researchers repeat previous studies in an identical way to see whether the findings can be replicated. Most researchers (and most funding bodies) want to carry out a new study of their own. Therefore, once they have reviewed the existing research a researcher needs to identify the gap to be filled by their study. This might be adding to the research in terms of a new sample, new measures or a new intervention, or it might be putting existing measures together in a novel way to ask a new research question. If the research is also informed by theory, then the gap in the literature may be testing a new theory or applying an existing theory in a novel way. My take on research is that it should not only fill a gap but also pass two key tests: 'So what'? and 'Was it worth it'? particularly if it is funded or using up valuable researcher time.

TYPES OF RESEARCH QUESTION

Once a researcher has identified a research area, they then need to refine their research question. Research generally involves one of six different types of questions. These are: (i) **exploratory questions** such as 'how do people feel'?, 'what do people think'?, and 'how do people say they behave'? Exploratory questions tend to be asked when very little research has been done before; (ii) **descriptive questions** include questions such as 'how many'?; 'how old'?; 'what kind of'? Descriptive questions mostly involve simple descriptions and often just use counting. They are asked to provide basic information; (iii) **differences questions** include a grouping variable in order look for differences between different groups. This grouping variable could be sex (men vs. women); age (old vs. young); group (patients vs. doctors); or health status (healthy vs. ill) which would lead to differences questions such as 'what are the differences between . . .'; 'men vs. women'; 'adults vs. children'; 'patients vs. doctors'; and 'diabetic (depressed/obese/cancer etc.) vs. non–diabetic (non–depressed/non–obese/no cancer, etc.)'; (iv) **association questions** explore the relationship between two or more variables and examine whether one variable increases as the other either increases or decreases. So we might ask 'as people get older to they get more happy'?, 'as people eat more to they get heavier'?, or 'as people get more aggressive does their number of friends decrease'?; (v) **causal questions** focus on causality such as 'does smoking cause cancer'?; 'does exercise prevent heart disease'?; 'does mixed sex education improve academic achievement'?; 'does having children cause divorce'?; 'does good parenting improve adult happiness'. These are probably the most commonly asked research questions. They are fundamental to our desire to make sense of our world as they involve trying to find the causal link between two or more variables; (vi) **process questions** tend to be asked after a causal question has identified how two or more variables are linked. Examples of process questions include 'what factors predict someone getting cancer if they smoke'?; 'how does exercise prevent heart disease'?; 'how does mixed sex education improvement academic achievement'?; 'what predicts when having children causes divorce'?; 'how does good parenting improve adult happiness'? Process questions are interested in mechanisms, sometimes called mediators or moderators. Have a look at Task 4 and decide which type of research question is which.

Task 4 What types of research question are these?

Are the following questions exploratory, descriptive, differences, associations, causal or process? (please circle)

Example	Types of question?
Does exercise reduce depression?	exp/desc/diff/ass/cau/pro
How many young people smoke cigarettes?	exp/desc/diff/ass/cau/pro
Is old age linked to loneliness?	exp/desc/diff/ass/cau/pro
Do condoms prevent the transmission of the AIDS virus?	exp/desc/diff/ass/cau/pro
How does exercise reduce depression?	exp/desc/diff/ass/cau/pro
How much screen time to children watch each day?	exp/desc/diff/ass/cau/pro
How many people eat 5 fruit and veg per day?	exp/desc/diff/ass/cau/pro
Does good weather change our mood?	exp/desc/diff/ass/cau/pro
Are men more aggressive than women?	exp/desc/diff/ass/cau/pro
Are people who watch more TV heavier?	exp/desc/diff/ass/cau/pro
How do young people feel about vaping?	exp/desc/diff/ass/cau/pro
Does screen time cause obesity?	exp/desc/diff/ass/cau/pro
Does poor parenting lead to increased screen time?	exp/desc/diff/ass/cau/pro
Does loneliness lead to depression?	exp/desc/diff/ass/cau/pro
How many people practice safe sex?	exp/desc/diff/ass/cau/pro

STUDYING VARIABLES

Research measures aspects of the world. These are called variables. Some of these might be **demographic variables** about each participant such as age, sex, weight, or social class; some might be **outcome variables** such as educational achievement, health status, or illness and some might be **predictor variables** such as beliefs, behaviour, or personality. In reality, most variables can be demographic, outcome, or predictor variables depending on the question being asked. Therefore, if we ask 'how heavy are our participants'?, weight is a demographic variable. However, if we ask 'does social class predict body weight'?, then weight becomes an outcome variable. Further, if we say 'does weight predict illness'?, then weight becomes a predictor variable. Therefore, what is important is the type of question being asked and where the variable sits in this question. In research, we often call the predictor variable the independent variable (IV) and the outcome variable the dependent variable (DV). This is because the status of the dependent variable DEPENDS upon the independent variable. Which variable is which varies according to the way in which a research question is asked. So if we ask 'does social class cause weight'?, weight is the DV as it is dependent on social class, which is the IV. This means that as social class changes so does weight. However, we could also ask 'does weight change social class'?, in which case weight has become the IV and social class has become the DV! Have a look at Task 5 and work out which variable is which.

Task 5 What types of variables are these?

In the following research questions, label which variables are demographics (D), predictor variables (IV) or the outcome variables (DV)

Example questions….
Does exercise reduce depression?
How do young people feel about vaping?
Is old age linked to loneliness?
How many young people smoke cigarettes?
How does exercise reduce depression?
How much screen time to children watch each day?
Does screen time cause obesity?
Does good weather change our mood?
Are men more aggressive than women?
Are people who watch more TV heavier?
Does poor parenting lead to increased screen time?
How many people eat 5 fruit and veg per day?
Does loneliness lead to depression?
Do condoms prevent the transmission of the AIDS virus?
How many people practice safe sex?

THE SAMPLE

Whether it is focused on health and illness, education, child development, or criminal behaviour most research is interested in the human condition. Yet no researcher can access all humans to find out how they all think, feel, behave, or just are. Studies therefore involve samples of people rather than all people. However, most researchers really want to know about more than just the people in their study and so they take the findings from their study and generalise them to the people not in their study. For example, I may have evaluated the impact of a drug compared to a placebo on 150 cancer patients from my clinic in Brighton but I want to be able to say that this drug works for patients with cancer elsewhere. Similarly, my study on surgery shows that obese people in my clinic in Leeds lose more weight than those who don't have surgery and I want to say that obese patients around the world would also benefit. Likewise, I know that children in my village get higher grades if they go to the mixed sex school rather than the single sex school but I genuinely believe this would be the case for all children everywhere. The degree to which researchers can make such claims is determined by the following factors illustrated in Figure 2.

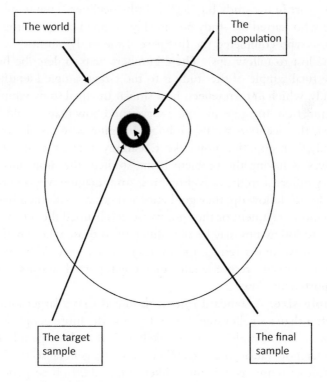

Figure 2 The sampling method.

The population: First, researchers need to identify who they want to generalise to. This could be cancer patients, obese patients, or school children. This is called the population and defines who the researchers are allowed to generalise to at the end of the study. Often this is done implicitly, if done at all.

Sampling method: Second, researchers need to identify a target sample from this population using a specific sampling method. Ideally this would be random (i.e. 1 in 10) or stratified (i.e. matched in age/sex/class, etc. to the population; also known as quota sampling). Both random and stratified sampling result in a sample that reflects the characteristics of the population. In reality, most people use opportunistic sampling (i.e. people who were available to do my study) or convenience (i.e. patients in my clinic in Brighton). Opportunistic and convenience sampling limit the right to generalise to the wider population as they generate samples that are less representative of this population.

Response rate: Next, once they have identified their target sample and completed the study researchers need to report their response rate and the numbers of people who dropped out from different stages of the study. This includes the number of people who were approached to take part in the study but declined (the decliners), the number of people who started the study but quickly dropped out (the drop outs), and those who completed the first part of the study but not the follow up (the lost to follow ups). These numbers help to describe how similar the final sample of the study is to the target sample identified for the study, which in turn reflects how similar the final study sample is to the population. Imagine an online survey and how many could have taken part; the decliners would be huge. Imagine why people might start a study then stop; they don't like it, it annoys them, they don't see themselves as having the problem being studied: the drop outs would be very different to the non-drop outs. And imagine why a person would be lost to follow up; they got better and got on with their lives needing no more treatment or they got worse and blamed the intervention; the lost to follow ups may be very different to those who stay in the study thus skewing the results. Ideally, response rates would be reported and high. In reality, response rates are rarely reported (and assumed low) or reported and low.

Sample size: A standard rule of thumb is that a larger sample size is better than a smaller one. This is because the more people a researcher has in their sample the more likely it is that these people reflect the wider population the researcher wants to generalise to. This makes intuitive sense, as it is more likely that 1,000 obese people are like all obese people than just 20. In addition, researchers are less likely to miss significant effects just because their sample is too small. This is known as a type 2 error or a false negative. There are, however, three problems with larger sample sizes. First, if the sample is too big then there is the chance that the researcher will find random associations that look significant when they are actually very small (if they are using p-values for significance testing – see below). This is known as a type 1 error or a false positive and is because small differences or associations can become significant differences or associations in large samples. To prevent this from happening researchers carry out a power calculation before the study to identify the optimal sample size and aim to match this. Often, however, researchers keep collecting data from more and more people until their effects turn significant. Second, just because a sample is bigger doesn't necessarily mean that it reflects the population as this depends upon the sampling method used. It is better to have a small sample with a high response rate rather than a larger sample with a very low response rate as this means it is not as skewed towards the kinds of people who take part in studies. Further, it is also better to have a smaller stratified sample that matches the population being generalised to than a larger convenience sample of people who just turned up. Third, small samples are better if the study aims to ask in depth questions of a few people. Qualitative studies therefore tend to have smaller samples. But these studies claim not to be interested in generalisability. Ideally, sample sizes would be large enough to avoid false negatives and small enough to avoid false positives and sampled in a way that is matched to the population. Generalisations can then be made. In reality, most researchers get whoever they can get!

Describing the sample: If any degree of generalisation is to be made from the sample to other similar people, we need to know who was in the sample. Researchers should therefore describe the participants' demographics such as age, sex, location, social class, education, height, weight, or anything that might be of relevance. In that way readers can see the kinds of people in the sample and therefore the kinds of people they can generalise to. This is obviously based on the (flawed) assumption that people with similar demographics are similar in other ways. Why not also describe their beliefs, emotions, or behaviour (as these are key for psychologists); their religion, culture, or income (for the sociologists or anthropologists) or their blood type, haemoglobin levels, or DNA (for the biologists). Describing the sample enables generalisations to be made to other 'similar' people. However, the definition of 'similar' is clearly determined by whatever you believe causes people to vary.

19

The variability of the variable being studied: The degree that a study's findings can be generalised also depends upon the variable being studied and whether it can be assumed to be consistent or to vary between people. Researchers in labs explore cells from people and assess whether one drug changes one set of cells more than another drug. They don't identify a population of people, sample from this population then sample their cells because it is assumed that all cells are the same regardless of who they come from. The variable being studied (the characteristic of the cell) is assumed to be homogenous, consistent, and unvaried and therefore it doesn't matter who it comes from or how it was accessed for the study. If researchers believe that their variable is similarly consistent then they might believe that they can generalise from their data without any of the steps above. So it might be assumed that all diabetic patients are the same (regardless of age, ethnic group, class, or gender) and that any sample will do and that obese people are all suffering from the same condition, so just find

Worked Example 2 Sampling method.

The stigma of mental illness (Angermeye & Matschinger, 2003).

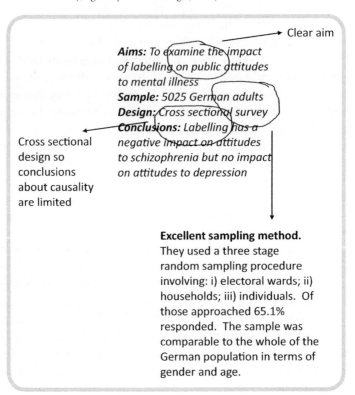

Clear aim

Aims: To examine the impact of labelling on public attitudes to mental illness
Sample: 5025 German adults
Design: Cross sectional survey
Conclusions: Labelling has a negative impact on attitudes to schizophrenia but no impact on attitudes to depression

Cross sectional design so conclusions about causality are limited

Excellent sampling method. They used a three stage random sampling procedure involving: i) electoral wards; ii) households; iii) individuals. Of those approached 65.1% responded. The sample was comparable to the whole of the German population in terms of gender and age.

some obese people. But it is unlikely that this is the case for the people that form the basis of most research questions. It is even unlikely that those who have diabetes or are obese are really the same in Nigeria as they are in Brighton. My gran was 100 when doctors tried to put her on drugs to lower her blood pressure when in fact no research has ever been done on 100-year-old women to find out what their blood pressure should be. Researchers might like to argue that their findings are generalisable outside of their study sample because their variables are homogenous. But mostly, it is unlikely that this is the case. A good sampling method is illustrated in Worked Example 2.

• •

THE STORY

The final basic feature common to all research is the story. Good research papers describe the relevant literature then identify a gap in the literature that leads to their research question. They then address the research question with the right research design, collect the data using the right approach to measurement, analyse the data asking the right questions and using the right approach to analysis, and then pull the findings together in the context of the relevant literature. Details of these different procedures are found in the next three chapters, which focus on knowing design, knowing measurement, and knowing data analysis. All research papers should also have a story that provides a coherent narrative to the data. Although there are many different research papers with many different ideas which have measured many different variables, I think that there are really only three possible types of story: (i) **And or yes stories:** An 'And' or 'Yes' story describes how a study adds to the existing literature. This might be by extending previous research to a new population, a new illness, a new problem, or using a new methodology but the story says 'Previous research shows xxx in Manchester. Is this the same in London? YES it is!' or 'Previous qualitative research shows xxxx AND this is also the case when assessed using quantitative methods' or 'Our intervention worked for patients with xxx. AND it also worked for those with xxx'. And/yes stories can be interesting but there has to be a point where we know enough and no longer need to keep extending the findings; (ii) **But stories:** 'But' stories are sometimes more controversial and involve going against the existing literature. This might be because previous research has not been replicated, a theory has been challenged, a finding has been shown not to extend to another population, or when using another methodology. For example, a 'But' story might say 'Previous research suggests that xxx relates to xxx BUT we found that it doesn't in our population indicating that it is not such a universal phenomenon as sometimes suggested', or 'The theory of xxx predicts

21

that xxx relates to xxx BUT we found no evidence to support this indicating that the theory is not as robust as often argued'. Not all but stories relate to negative findings. For example, 'previous research found that xxx caused xxx. BUT we found that xxx was a much better predictor'. This is also a but story but with a positive finding; (iii) **How stories:** Stories which focus on 'How' tend to be about process, mechanisms, or are in depth and exploratory. At times, this is because the research has already identified a causal link and so a HOW question explores how this link works. For example, 'Research indicates that social class predicts lung cancer. HOW does this work? We found that smoking is the best explanation of this association' or 'Research shows that mindfulness reduces absenteeism from work. Our research indicates that this is due to mindfulness helping people deal with stress'. At times this is also because very little is known already. Examples of exploratory stories might be 'We explored HOW people make sense of divorce. The results showed xxxx' or 'Post polio syndrome is a little studied condition. We found that people living with it experience xxx'.

IN SUMMARY

The first step to thinking critically about research involves knowing methodology before it can be critically analysed. This first involves knowing the basics and this chapter has described these basics in terms of finding a research area, types of research questions, the sample, studying variables, and the story. All of these are fundamental to any research study. The next chapter will explore the use of different research designs.

3

KNOWING DESIGN

OVERVIEW

The research design for any study is key as it frames the meaning of the data and limits any conclusions that can be made. There are a number of different designs used for research. This chapter will describe qualitative, cross-sectional, case control, longitudinal, and experimental (trial) designs. It will also illustrate how they address links between variables, the problem of alternative explanations and outline their strengths and limitations. Next it will take a simple question 'Does aspirin work'? and illustrate the extent to which each research design can answer this one question.

DIFFERENT DESIGNS

The range of possible research designs are shown in Figure 3 and described below with a focus on the links between variables, the possibility of alternative explanations for any findings and the strengths and limitations of each design.

QUALITATIVE DESIGNS

Qualitative designs are an inductive and 'bottom-up' approach. This means that they are exploratory and used when little is already known on the subject. Therefore, the ideas emerge 'up' from the data rather than being imposed 'down' by the researcher. Interviews and focus groups are both types of qualitative methods and are used to enable new understandings about the world to emerge. So if very little is known about how patients feel about cancer treatment, how children feel about going to a mixed school, or how the general public feel about their new Prime Minister researchers might carry out interviews and analyse what people say. There are several different types of qualitative data analysis including thematic analysis, discourse analysis, narrative analysis, and conversational analysis. These all vary in their theoretical perspectives and the ways in which data is coded. They all start, however, from

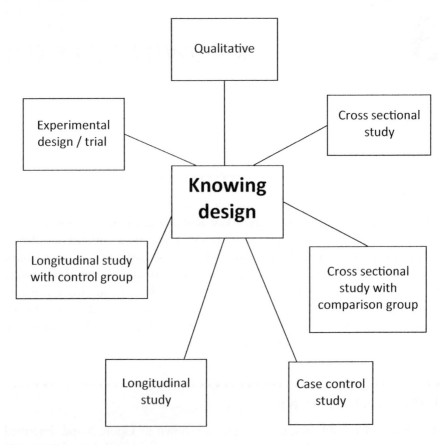

Figure 3 Knowing design.

the perspective of knowing very little and venturing into new territories to generate rich and novel data.

> **The links between variables:** As qualitative methods are inductive and all data comes 'up' from the participants any links between variables are also made by the participants. Therefore, if we ask participants 'do you think the exercises we gave you helped your pain get better' and they say 'yes the exercises made my back feel a lot better' they are making the link between the independent variable (the exercise) and the dependent variable (pain). This data tells us that they believe that the exercises worked and have experienced the pain as getting better. This is useful. But because they have made the link between the variables themselves it doesn't tell us whether the exercises really worked. It just tells us that they think they worked.

Alternative explanations: Just because participants believe there is a link between variables doesn't mean that there really is a link between these variables. Therefore, in the scenario described above participants may believe that the exercise helped their pain but this link could be due to a multitude of alternative explanations. For example, the participant might have wanted the exercises to work or expected them to work, because they had paid for them, made a lot of effort to do them, or liked their exercise instructor. This is the 'placebo effect' (meaning 'to please'). Alternatively, something else might have happened alongside the exercises: the weather may have warmed up, they may have changed their mattress, started walking to work rather than driving, or simply increased their dose of painkillers to mask the pain. These are known as third factors or confounding variables and provide a host of alternative explanations for the link participants report between two variables.

Strengths: Qualitative methods are in their element when researchers have no hypotheses or theories to test. They can be carried out with relatively small samples and can generate rich, novel, and surprising data. They enable a subject area to be studied in depth and can be used in their own right, as the basis of further quantitative research or to add richness to existing quantitative research.

Limitations: Because of their sampling methods, qualitative data is not generalisable beyond any specific data set. The results therefore tell us how the participants of the study feel but not how all similar people feel. In addition, qualitative data does not reveal the 'truth' about the world, but what people think that truth is. Therefore, if a study shows that children in a mixed school feel that they don't do as well academically as those in single sexed schools this means that they THINK this is the case rather than this IS the case. Likewise, if people feel eating broccoli prevents cancer this is also their BELIEF rather than evidence that broccoli DOES actually prevent cancer. Qualitative data provides people's stories and narratives about truth rather than the truth.

CROSS-SECTIONAL SURVEYS

Cross-sectional surveys involve asking questions online or using a paper questionnaire. They are a means to access a wider population than qualitative methods and can generate data that is more generalisable. They cannot generate such in depth data but are useful for finding out what a larger sample think and do, and for creating data that can be quantified. For example, if you wanted to know if exercise helped with back pain a study could sample 500 people in a more stratified manner and ask them 'does exercise help with your back pain'? The results would then show that 65% of those sampled believed that exercise helped pain.

> **Links between variables:** Although cross-sectional surveys generate quantitative data they are still asking participants to make their own links between variables. So when asked in a survey about the impact of the exercises, participants are still working out whether they believe that the exercises impact upon their back problems. Accordingly, all we know from this data is that people think exercises are good for back pain.
>
> **Alternative explanations:** As with qualitative methods, there is a multitude of alternative explanations as to why people might want to link the two variables of exercise and back pain together and believe that the exercises worked. These include placebo effects (wanting them to work, having paid, and liking the instructor) or a host of third factor variables such as the weather, a lovely holiday, or simple painkillers.
>
> **Strengths:** A cross sectional survey enables access to a large sample and the collection of quantitative data.
>
> **Limitations:** The data is purely descriptive.

CROSS-SECTIONAL SURVEY WITH A COMPARISON GROUP

A cross-sectional survey with a comparison group involves asking questions in a questionnaire and can generate large-scale quantitative data. It also enables comparisons to be made between different groups. This means that researchers can study the difference between men vs. women, old vs. young, ill vs. healthy, or teachers vs. pupils. It also means that if researchers want to know the impact of a specific intervention they can compare those who have had the intervention vs. those who have not. For this design, the comparison group becomes the control group. For many studies if the variable you are studying is common then data can be collected from a large sample, a question can be included to split the participants into two or more groups, and then comparisons are made. Therefore, if you were interested in sex differences in exercise behaviour you could send a questionnaire to 500 people, ask them their sex (male vs. female), ask them how much they exercise (e.g. hours per week) and be confident that you would have enough men and women to split the sample into two fairly equal groups for comparison. Likewise, if you wanted to know differences in depression between healthy weight and overweight people, a large-scale survey asking people about their weight and mood would generate a fairly balanced split by body weight to look for group differences. Similarly, if you were interested in whether people who get more coughs and colds

Worked Example 3 A cross-sectional study with comparison group.

Gender differences in health (Macintyre, Hunt, & Sweeting, 1996).

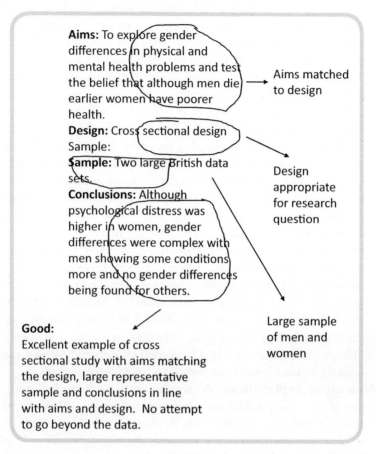

Aims: To explore gender differences in physical and mental health problems and test the belief that although men die earlier women have poorer health.

Aims matched to design

Design: Cross sectional design
Sample:

Sample: Two large British data sets.

Conclusions: Although psychological distress was higher in women, gender differences were complex with men showing some conditions more and no gender differences being found for others.

Design appropriate for research question

Good:
Excellent example of cross sectional study with aims matching the design, large representative sample and conclusions in line with aims and design. No attempt to go beyond the data.

Large sample of men and women

take more antibiotics you could ask for data on these two variables, split the sample into high vs. low users of antibiotics, and see if the two groups differ in their number of minor illnesses. These studies could show that men do more exercise than women, that those who are overweight are more depressed than those of healthy weight, and that high users of antibiotics get more coughs and colds. A good cross-sectional survey with a comparison group is shown in Worked Example 3.

Links between variables: In a cross-sectional study with a comparison group the two variables are no longer put together by the participant but by the researcher; the participant doesn't tell us 'my sex is linked to my smoking', 'my mood is linked to my weight', or 'my coughs and colds are linked to my antibiotic use'. Instead, the researcher separates these two variables into two separate measures and then puts them together in the analysis. For example, one measure would assess sex (are you male or female?) and another measure would assess smoking (do you smoke?). This means that we can be clearer that these two variables are linked together rather than just having participants tell us that they think they are. Just because two variables are linked, however, does not mean that one causes the other. With cross-sectional data there is always the fundamental problem of reverse causality as both variables have been measured at the same time. So being depressed may cause overweight, but it is also possible that being overweight causes people to feel depressed as they feel stigmatised. Likewise, having lots of coughs and cold may cause an increase in antibiotic use, but it is also highly likely that taking lots of antibiotics damages the immune system increasing a person's susceptibility to catching minor illnesses. Reverse causality is a problem central to many research studies. It is also a fundamental error that we make in our everyday lives whenever we see two events happen together and assume that they are not only connected but that one has caused the other. The only time reverse causality isn't a problem for cross-sectional studies is when one of the variables is in the past and unlikely to be impacted by the variable being measured. I once examined a PhD that showed that being involved in a drug related gang in Nigeria was related to having more siblings (mean number 13). I conceded that ending up in a gang was unlikely to have caused the person to have lots of siblings.

Alternative explanations: A cross-sectional study with a comparison group may show a difference between the groups. However, there is always a multitude of alternative explanations for these findings. This is known as the third factor problem and highlights the role of confounding variables. It might be that those who take more antibiotics have more coughs and colds. However, it could also be that those who take more antibiotics have other illnesses such as cancer which make them immune suppressed and that is why they get more coughs and colds. Similarly, depression may cause weight gain but it is also likely that those who are depressed eat more and are more sedentary and it is these factors that result in someone becoming overweight. Alternatively, it might simply be that people who are depressed are more likely to be women and women are more likely to be overweight. Sometimes these third factors variables (or confounding variables) help explain the relationship between the two original variables (i.e. the link between depression and obesity is explained by eating behaviour). These reflect the mechanisms or process by which the two variables are linked. Sometimes these third factor variables are actually the real predictor variables but just making it look as if the original variables are linked (depression doesn't really cause obesity, it's all due to being a woman).

Strengths: A cross-sectional design with a comparison group enables data to be collected from a large and more representative sample so that the findings are more generalisable. It separates out variables from each other in the measures and then puts them back together in the analysis, which means any link between variables is more than just participants believing there is a link. Further, they are useful designs when the variables are quite common.

Limitations: The two key limitations of cross-sectional designs with a comparison group are (i) reverse causality and (ii) the third factor problem. As variables are all measured at the same time it is impossible to say which caused which as causality can always go either way. In addition, the variables may not be linked at all but simply due to other third factors or confounding variables that may or may not have been measured.

CASE–CONTROL STUDY

The case control design is very similar to a cross-sectional design with a comparison group but used when one of the variables being studied is rare. For example, if I wanted to assess differences between women who had high versus low body dissatisfaction, I could send out a questionnaire to 500 women, measure body dissatisfaction (and a number of other factors such as mood, eating behaviour, addiction, etc.) and I could safely predict that body dissatisfaction would be common enough for me to have two fairly equal groups of high and low body dissatisfaction. However, if I wanted to assess differences in these same variables between those with an eating disorder and those without, my study might only come back with 1% with an eating disorder so I would have five in one group and 495 in the other. This is the strength of a case–control study. For a case–control study, the researcher first accesses a sample of the selected cases (i.e. people with an eating disorder). They then find a comparison group of participants who are MATCHED in key variables but DON'T have an eating disorder. The researcher can then compare the two equal sized groups on the relevant variables (mood, eating behaviour, addiction, etc.).

The key problem with a case–control study, however, is deciding which variables to match the two groups on because whatever you match them on cannot be the variable that you think they might differ on! This is illustrated by the classic case–control study on smoking and lung cancer carried out by Doll and Hill (1950, 1956). Doll and Hill wanted to know what caused lung cancer so they used a case–control study to identify their rare participants (those with lung cancer) and then compared them with a matched group of patients without lung cancer. They didn't know that smoking was going to be their key finding but they matched them on basic demographics (i.e. age, sex, etc.) not smoking. Had they matched them on smoking (which given that about 60% of the population smoked at that time could have happened) we would never have known that smoking was linked to lung cancer. However, they didn't match them on smoking and so we now know that smoking was what differentiated between those with lung cancer and those without. Not that people believed them at the time!

> **Links between variables:** As with a cross-sectional design with a comparison group, in a case–control study the researcher makes the links between variables in the analysis. But as variables are measured at the same time the problem of reverse causality remains, as causality can go either way (does an eating disorder cause lowered mood or does lowered mood cause an eating disorder?).
>
> **Alternative explanations:** With a case control design, several possible alternative explanations are ruled out through the process of matching the groups (as the groups are the same on these variables). But, the third factor problem remains as there is always the possibility that any link between variables is really a product of other variables that were not used for matching the groups. It could be that people who smoke also work in industries with high rates of chemicals and it is these chemicals that cause lung cancer, not smoking. It isn't.
>
> **Strengths:** A case–control study is a useful design when one variable is rare and it enables comparisons between matched groups. The matching helps to control for a number of third factors.
>
> **Limitations:** The case control design cannot solve the problem of reverse causality. Nor can it control for all possible third factors as not everything can be measured and even if it is measured not everything can be matched for.

A LONGITUDINAL STUDY

A longitudinal study (also called a cohort study or a repeated measures study) involves collecting data over a period of time. This means that researchers can observe how variables change from baseline (time one) to a follow up which might be minutes, months, or years into the future. This is key if we are to understand the longer-term impact of any intervention. For example, if you wanted to explore the impact of weight loss surgery on weight loss you could collect weight data before and after the operation and then at 6 months, 12 months, and 2 years. Likewise, if you were interested in whether exercise helped people with back pain you could tell everyone to do the exercises and

Worked Example 4 A longitudinal study.

Crime deterrence: evidence from the London 2011 riots (Bell, Jaitman, & Machin, 2014).

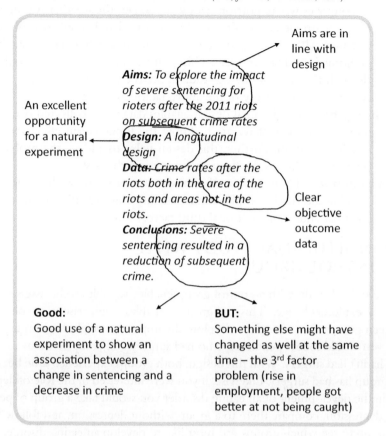

measure their back pain before and after the exercises and for the next six weeks. A good longitudinal study is shown in Worked Example 4.

Links between variables: A longitudinal design enables links to be made between variables as the variables are measured separately then put together in the analysis. But, the main benefit of adding time into a study is that it solves the problem of reverse causality as things in the future cannot cause things in the past. If you want to know the link between depression and weight gain, and have measured depression at baseline then weight gain five years later and find a link, it cannot be argued that the future weight gain caused the depression five years ago.

Alternative explanations: With a longitudinal design, the third factor problem remains as many confounding variables could explain a

31

change over time. Depression at baseline may be linked to weight gain by five years but there may be other explanations such as people moved to countries where portion sizes were bigger, the weather was dreadful and they stopped exercising, or TV improved and people became more sedentary. PLUS, by adding in time the researcher has added in an additional third factor: time. Things just change over time. Nothing to do with the variables being studied. So, the reason people lose weight may not be due to any of the above factors, just time.

Strengths: A longitudinal design enables data to be collected over time. This is important if we are to know the longer-term effectiveness of any intervention. Further, this design helps to address the problem of reverse causality, as the future cannot cause the past.

Limitations: There remains the third factor problem, as there are many possible alternative explanations for any finding. PLUS, the design itself has added an additional third factor: time.

A LONGITUDINAL STUDY WITH A CONTROL GROUP

A longitudinal study with a control group enables variables to be assessed over time to explore change. This design also enables comparisons to be made between groups. For example, to explore the impact of weight loss surgery over time you would follow people up who had surgery and compare them to those who hadn't had surgery. With this design, both groups experience time but only one group has had surgery. Likewise, if you were interested in the role of depression in the development of an eating disorder you would take a group of people with depression, compare them to a group without depression, and follow both groups up to see which groups was most like to develop an eating disorder.

Links between variables: The longitudinal design solves the problem of reverse causality, as what happens in the future cannot cause what has happened in the past. From this design, you can make a stronger claim about causality.

Alternative explanations: The longitudinal design adds an additional third factor: time. Adding the control group solves the problem of time as the third factor as both groups have had time and therefore any difference between the group cannot be due to time. However, many other differences could still explain any findings. Both groups may have been different in age, sex, eating behaviour, smoking, hobbies, attitudes, outlook on life, childhood experiences, etc. Possible third factors are never ending.

Strengths: This solves the reverse causality problem.

Limitations: It does not solve the problem of the third factor and introduces the extra problem of time.

EXPERIMENTAL DESIGN

For an experimental design (or randomised control trial [RCT], experiment, or trial) participants are randomly allocated to one or more arms (often called conditions, interventions, groups). One arm then receives an intervention (or treatment, or task) whilst the other arm receives a control intervention (or treatment or task). Measures are then taken at baseline and after the intervention. For example, to evaluate the impact of nicotine patches on smoking cessation, smokers would be randomly allocated to receive either nicotine patches or placebo patches and their smoking behaviour would be measured before and after to assess any change. Likewise, to assess the effectiveness of exercise for the treatment of depression, people with depression would be allocated either to carry out exercise or not and changes in depression would be measured. Sometimes there are several arms to a trial (no exercise vs. light exercise vs. regular exercise) and sometimes there are several follow up time points. The following issues arise with RCTs and experimental designs.

Randomisation ensures that participants end up in each arm purely by chance. It should be done using a random number generator and not by any factor that might have some order to it. Some factors might seem random but actually have order: alphabetically by surname (but some initials are more common in some cultures than others); time of day (those who come earlier might be morning people); by entry into study (those who sign up earlier might be keener). Randomisation should also be done by a third party to avoid bias and before the point of telling the participant which arm they are in. This is to avoid researcher bias as it is quite possible that the researcher could chose who to give the active intervention to on the basis on who they think would most benefit. Therefore, if the participant arrives and they seem highly motivated the researcher might think 'I will put them in the exercise group' as they are most likely to do the exercises. This obviously undermines the process of randomisation as those in the exercise group will end up not only doing exercise but also be more motivated. Randomisation can be checked by comparing the different groups at baseline on whatever variables have been measured (age, sex, weight, illness history, etc.). This cannot account for those variables that haven't been measured. Randomisation becomes more effective the larger the sample.

One problem for researchers using this design is the **choice of control intervention,** as they need to make sure they control for everything other than the active part of the intervention they are testing. Sometimes interventions are compared to treatment as usual (TAU) if the intervention is new and predicted just to be better than whatever is routinely available. But, often the question is more specific than that. Therefore, a nicotine patch needs

33

to be compared to a placebo patch as opposed to no patch as simply wearing a patch may have an effect. Likewise, a 60-minute consultation with a specialised dietician to discuss dietary changes needs to be compared with a 60-minute chat with someone else, as simply chatting for an hour might be an active intervention. Looking at images of idealised women to see if they impact on body image needs to be compared to images of something else as simply starring at images may cause change.

When using the RCT or experimental design it is common to **blind the participants** and **blind the researchers** as to the arm of the trial the participant is in if possible. When both are blinded this is called a **double blinded trial**. This reduces the risk of expectancy effects or social desirability effects with participants showing change because they know what is expected of them and researchers changing how they record and analyse data. Sometimes, however, this is not possible when interventions are obvious to all concerned.

Experiments or trials can be analysed using either **Intention to Treat (ITT)** analysis or **Explanatory Analysis (EA)** also called a **Proof of Principal (POP)** analysis that differ in terms of the denominator used. For an ITT analysis, all participants who are offered the intervention are included in the analysis even if they didn't attend or dropped out. This perspective is a pragmatic analysis and asks 'Would the intervention be effective in the real world'? and takes into account uptake rates and the reality of delivering an intervention. Therefore, if a new drug were offered to 1000 patients and only 200 were happy to take it; the analysis would use the 1000 patients to account for the fact that in the real world people don't seem to like the drug. When using an ITT analysis there is often a lot of missing data due to people either not taking part at all or dropping out which need to be imputed to carry out the analysis. This can be done using different approaches such as carrying their baseline data through to follow up or using the mean data of the sample to replace missing data. ITT analyses are used in clinical trials. In contrast, EA (and POP) analyses just include those participants who take part and complete the study. This approach asks 'Does this intervention work for those people who do the intervention'? Therefore, if 1000 are offered a drug and only 200 take it, the study would use these 200 to see if the drug made a difference when it was actually taken. EA analysis is always used in experiments in the laboratory. It is also often the first analysis carried out for trials before an ITT analysis. An excellent RCT is shown in Worked Example 5.

> **Links between variables:** The different variables have been separated in the measures and put together by the researcher. Further,

Worked Example 5 Randomised controlled trial.

Effect of corticosteroids on death after head injury (Roberts et al. (CRASH trial), 2004).

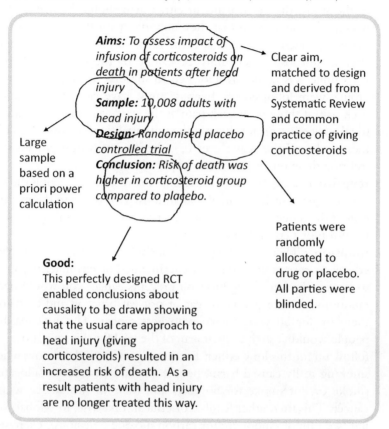

Aims: To assess impact of infusion of corticosteroids on death in patients after head injury

Sample: 10,008 adults with head injury

Design: Randomised placebo controlled trial

Conclusion: Risk of death was higher in corticosteroid group compared to placebo.

Clear aim, matched to design and derived from Systematic Review and common practice of giving corticosteroids

Large sample based on a priori power calculation

Patients were randomly allocated to drug or placebo. All parties were blinded.

Good:
This perfectly designed RCT enabled conclusions about causality to be drawn showing that the usual care approach to head injury (giving corticosteroids) resulted in an increased risk of death. As a result patients with head injury are no longer treated this way.

they have been separated by time. This solves the problem of reverse causality and enables a strong statement concluding that one variable (the independent or predictor variable) caused another variable (the dependent or outcome variable). In addition, the experimental design means that the independent variable has been manipulated and changed (i.e. exercise or no exercise). Any change in the dependent variable should therefore be a result of the change in the independent variable.

Alternative explanations: Follow up data introduces the third factor of time but this has now been solved by the control group as both groups had time for variables to change. For a longitudinal design with a control group, many other possible alternative explanations remain. But these are all solved by the process of randomisation. Because a single sample at baseline has been randomly allocated to the different arms of the study, the participants in either arm should be matched. This matching should mean that they only differ on the one key variable: the independent variable that is the focus of the study. So weight loss after weight loss surgery must be caused by the surgery if the original sample was randomly allocated to surgery, or not, and then both groups were followed up. Exercise must have caused a reduction in back pain if those with back pain at the start were randomly allocated to take exercises or not. Even if the potential third factors haven't been measured (and they can't ever be), the randomisation process should still rule these out as alternative explanations.

Strengths: The experimental design has many strengths, as it is the strongest design for making causal conclusions. This is due to the manipulation of the independent variable, the process of randomisation, and the inclusion of a control group.

Limitations: There are many occasions when it is neither feasible nor ethical to carry out a trial or experiment. For example, if you want to know whether eating broccoli prevents cancer you would need to randomly allocate people to eat or not eat broccoli and then follow them up for 50 years to see who gets cancer. This isn't feasible as people wouldn't stick to their arm of the trial for this long, nor can we follow up for this long either. Further if you wanted to know whether smoking really caused harm, people would be randomly allocated to smoke or not smoke for 50 years and then we would see who got cancer. This isn't either feasible or ethical. Likewise, for global warming (we cannot randomise for carbon dioxide emissions), exercise and heart disease (how much exercise/would they stick to it?/how long) or thalidomide and birth deformities (not ethical if it might cause any harm at all). For many research questions, we have to take the best available evidence generated by imperfect research studies and pool this together to make the best conclusions we can. Further, the results from a RCT or experiment are limited in their generalisability due to the samples used.

A RANDOMISED RANDOMISED CONTROL TRIAL

The RCT or experimental design is heralded as the gold standard of research designs for questions about causality as it solves the problem of reverse causality and alternative explanations. It therefore allows strong statements to be made about causal links between variables. But the one flaw remaining with this design is sampling and whether the results from an RCT or experiment can be generalised. Most RCTs are carried out in one clinic in one town. Some are multi-centred and carried out in several towns. Occasionally RCTs are also carried out in several towns in several countries. But mostly they aren't which limits their generalisability. Furthermore, the study sample is very rarely randomly sampled from the population to be generalised to, meaning that the study sample is unlikely to reflect the wider population. So, when research states drug A works for patients with diabetes, what the researchers really mean is that drug A works for THE people with diabetes in this trial; it might also work for other people like the people in the trial, but we don't know if it works for other people with diabetes who differ in age, ethnic group, etc. Given that most trials are carried out on people who chose to consent to take part in trials, who live near a research centre, are aged between 30–60, not pregnant, and are often selected as those most likely to benefit, the results cannot be generalised to anyone who doesn't match this profile. Researchers should therefore carry out a randomised randomised control trial, but they never do, as the funding is not available.

The research design is key to any study as it frames the meaning of the data and limits any conclusions that can be drawn. This chapter has described designs ranging from qualitative approaches with their emphasis on exploration and depth through quantitative designs including cross-sectional design, longitudinal designs, and the experimental design (or RCT). They all have their strengths and limitations and vary in the way they address the links between variables and the host of alternative explanations. To illustrate the uses of each design they will now be used to answer one research question: 'Does aspirin work'?

• •

USING THE DIFFERENT DESIGNS: 'DOES ASPIRIN WORK'?

If a researcher wanted to know 'Does aspirin work'? they could carry out a series of studies using all the different designs described previously. These designs would frame the meaning of the data and limit the conclusions that could be made as follows. They would also have different implications for solving the problems of reverse causality and the third factor problem. This is illustrated in Figure 4 and described below.

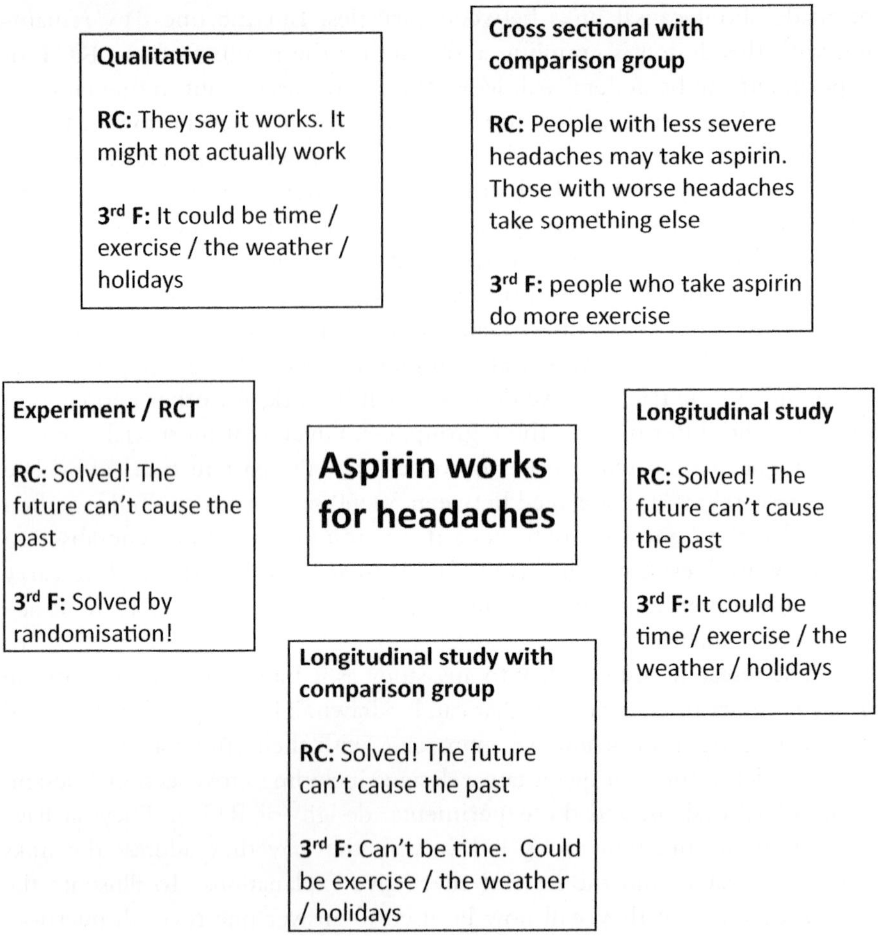

Qualitative

RC: They say it works. It might not actually work

3rd F: It could be time / exercise / the weather / holidays

Cross sectional with comparison group

RC: People with less severe headaches may take aspirin. Those with worse headaches take something else

3rd F: people who take aspirin do more exercise

Experiment / RCT

RC: Solved! The future can't cause the past

3rd F: Solved by randomisation!

Aspirin works for headaches

Longitudinal study

RC: Solved! The future can't cause the past

3rd F: It could be time / exercise / the weather / holidays

Longitudinal study with comparison group

RC: Solved! The future can't cause the past

3rd F: Can't be time. Could be exercise / the weather / holidays

Figure 4 Are the conclusions justified?

(The problems of reverse causality (RC) and third factors (3rd F)).

A QUALITATIVE STUDY

Method: Interview 20 people and ask them about their experiences of taking aspirin.

Results: People feel that aspirin is particularly good for headaches.

Conclusion: Aspirin works for headaches.

Are the conclusions justified? No. Results show people THINK aspirin works for headaches but this is just their narrative and view. This doesn't mean it does work.

What the findings really show: People feel aspirin works. This could be interesting if nothing was known about aspirin or if we wanted to know how people experience aspirin.

A CROSS-SECTIONAL SURVEY

Method: Collect 500 questionnaires asking whether people think aspirin works.

Results: 75% think aspirin works.

Conclusion: Aspirin works for the majority of people.

Are the conclusions justified? No. The results show that the majority of people in this study think aspirin works. Again, it is just their view.

What the findings really show: That the majority of people believe aspirin work. This could be useful as a first line of evidence.

A CROSS-SECTIONAL SURVEY WITH A COMPARISON GROUP

Methods: Take 500 people with headaches and compare those who take aspirin to those who do not take aspirin.

Results: Those who take aspirin have shorter and milder headaches.

Conclusion: Aspirin reduces the length and severity of headaches.

Are the conclusions justified? No. Aspirin may make headaches milder and shorter, or those who take aspirin already have milder headaches which are shorter whilst those with longer and more severe headaches may take other medication, or believing in aspirin makes headaches shorter and milder, or people who take aspirin also do exercise and gets lots of fresh air and that is what makes their headaches better.

What the results really show: Taking aspirin may be associated with shorter and milder headaches but this isn't causal and may be due to many possible third factors.

A CASE–CONTROL STUDY

Methods: Find people with headaches who take aspirin and compare them to a group of people who have headaches but don't take aspirin and match them on age, sex, ethnicity, and headache history.

Results: Those who take aspirin have shorter and milder headaches.

Conclusion: Aspirin reduces the length and severity of headaches.

Are these conclusions justified? No. Aspirin may help with headaches, or those who take aspirin may have shorter and less severe headaches whilst those with longer and more severe headaches may take other medication, or believing in aspirin makes headaches shorter and less severe, or people who take aspirin differ from those who don't on hundreds of factors that weren't matched for in the matching process such as doing exercise.

What do the findings really show: That taking aspirin is linked with shorter and less severe headaches, but we don't know if this is causal and this link may in fact be a product of many other possible third factors.

A LONGITUDINAL STUDY

Method: Find 200 people with headaches, give them aspirin, and follow them up.

Results: The headaches go away.

Conclusions: Aspirin makes headaches go away.

Are these conclusions justified? No. It could just be time that made the headaches better, or people could have taken more exercise as well as aspirin, or it could have been the holidays, or they could have believed that aspirin works which helped the headaches.

What the findings really show: Headaches change over time. This change coincided with taking aspirin but this association is not causal and could easily just be a coincidence.

A LONGITUDINAL DESIGN WITH A CONTROL GROUP

Methods: Take 200 people with headaches and give half aspirin. Follow them all up.

Results: Those who took aspirin had shorter and less severe headaches.

Conclusions: Aspirin works.

Are the conclusions justified? No. The change in headaches can no longer just be the effect of time but the two groups may have been different in a multitude of other ways. Those who took aspirin may have all been women, older, more active, or all very keen on meditation.

What the results really show: Taking aspirin is associated with shorter and less severe headaches. This doesn't mean it causes headaches to get shorter and less severe. There are many other alternative explanations.

● ●

A RANDOMISED CONTROL TRIAL (OR EXPERIMENT)

Methods: Take 200 people with headaches and randomly allocate them to receive aspirin or a placebo pill. Follow them up.
Results: Those who took aspirin had shorter and less severe headaches.
Conclusions: Aspirin works for headaches.
Are the conclusions justified? Yes, as much as they ever can be. However, these findings may not be true for other people who are not like the ones in the study.
What the results really show: Aspirin makes patients in the study sample report that their headaches are shorter and less severe than those who had the placebo pill. but, it is likely that this wasn't the case for all patients in the trial. It is also unlikely that this will be the case for all people everywhere who get headaches.

● ●

A RANDOMISED RANDOMISED CONTROL TRIAL

Methods: Take the population of the world. Identify all those with headaches. Identify a random sample from this population that is stratified to match the population. Then randomly allocate them to receive aspirin or a placebo pill. Follow them up.
Results: Those who take aspirin had shorter and less severe headaches.
Conclusions: Aspirin works for headaches.
Are the conclusions justified? Yes, as much as they ever can be.
What the results really show: Aspirin makes headaches shorter and less severe. but there will always be variability in the results as nothing works for all the people all the time.

IN SUMMARY

The first step in thinking critically about research is knowing methodology. This chapter has focused on research design, which frames the data and limits the conclusions that can be drawn from the findings. This chapter has described the core research designs, highlighted their implications for making links between variables, and the possibility of alternative explanations. It has also illustrated how using different designs to answer one research question 'does aspirin work' highlights their strengths and weaknesses. All designs have their use. There is no one design that is always better than the others. The key is to match the research design to the research question being asked and to draw conclusions from the data that are justified by the design used. Knowing measurement is also important. This is the focus of the next chapter.

4

KNOWING
MEASUREMENT

....

OVERVIEW

Researchers measure a range of variables. Those interested in laboratory science may measure cell replication or decay and the impact of a new drug upon this process. For those interested in clinical medicine, blood pressure, weight, or glucose metabolism may be what they measure whilst epidemiologists focus on illness prevalence and incidence. Such research involves questions such as 'How many cells are there'?, 'What is their rate of decay'?, 'What is an individual's level of insulin production'?, or 'How many new cases of cancer are there each year'? These questions require a simple process of measurement as the cells and cases are counted and the numbers shown on weighing scales or blood pressure machines are recorded. The machines may need to be calibrated but no one asks the questions 'How do you know'?, 'Are you sure'? or 'Says who'? What it is, is what is measured and measurement is simple (or so they tell us!). For many research studies, however, measurement is much more complex. This chapter will explore different types of measurement, theories of measurement, and how we can check the usefulness of any measurement tool focusing on conceptualisation, operationalisation, reliability, and validity. These different issues will then be illustrated in terms of how we can measure one variable: health status.

....

DIFFERENT TYPES OF MEASUREMENT

Researchers measure everything whether it is blood cells or stomach volume, social class or education, political views or prejudice, life satisfaction or happiness, or diet, exercise, and smoking behaviours. There are many different approaches to measurement that can be classified as either objective or subjective. This will be illustrated with measures of adherence to medication.

OBJECTIVE MEASURES

Objective measures are usually quantified and often involve a level of technical input such as blood counts, x-rays or scans, or covert observations by the researcher. Objective measures are considered uncontaminated by bias, recall problems, issues of social desirability, and self-report. They each still have their costs and benefits. Examples of objective measures of adherence to medication are: (i) **Observation:** Researchers or clinicians can directly observe how many pills a patient takes. This is accurate but time consuming and not always feasible; (ii) **Blood or urine samples:** These can be taken to assess blood levels of the drug. This is objective but costly, time consuming, and varies according to how drugs are metabolised by different individuals; (iii) **Pill counting:** Patients are asked to bring their remaining pills in to be counted. This requires face-to-face meetings which are time consuming and inconvenient and patients may throw away pills in order to appear adherent; (iv) **Electronic monitors:** Pill bottles can contain a computer chip to record each time the bottle is opened. This can provide detailed information about drug taking. However, it assumes that a pill is taken each time the bottle is opened and is expensive; (v) **Assessing prescriptions:** Records can be made of when patients ask for new prescriptions. This assumes that patients have taken the used pills and that they ask for a new prescription exactly when they have run out.

Examples of other objective measures include blood type, scanning data, height, weight, temperature, and age. In the social sciences objective measures may be taken of behaviours such as smoking, exercise, alcohol consumption, or diet through methods such as measuring saliva (for smoking); using an electronic wearable device that detects movement (for exercise); accessing sales receipts from supermarkets or bank accounts; covert observation of participants in their everyday lives in cafes or at work; or overt observation in a laboratory setting.

SUBJECTIVE MEASURES

Subjective measures rely upon self-report and are therefore open to bias by the participants, problems of recall, or issues of social desirability. Subjective measures include interviews and questionnaires. Some constructs, however, can only be measured using subjective measures as they are subjective constructs. Examples of these include beliefs, attitudes, experiences, emotions, and symptoms. Subjective measures of adherence to medication are as follows: (i) **Self-report:** Patients can rate their own adherence during either an interview or using a questionnaire. This is inexpensive and simple but may be contaminated by recall problems and social desirability. It is possible to 'normalise' non-adherence as a means to reduce social desirability by stating 'People sometimes say that it is hard to always take their medication. How often do you take yours'? However, this may in fact promote non-adherence; (ii) **Unidimensional:** Some self-report measures are unidimensional and only focus on one aspect of a given construct. For adherence, an example of this would be to measure adherence to a specific medicine; (iii) **Multidimensional:** If the particular construct being measured is conceptualised in a more multidimensional way then a more multidimensional measure would be used. If adherence was conceptualised as 'adherence to health related behaviours' the measure would need to include items relating not only to medication, but also diet, smoking, exercise, and sleep.

Examples of other subjective measures include political views, pain, tiredness, depression, and prejudice. These are all states of mind and can therefore be measured using subjective measurement tools. Different types of measurement are shown in Worked Example 6.

Worked Example 6 Types of measurement.

Increasing donor registration through black churches (Andrews et al., 2012).

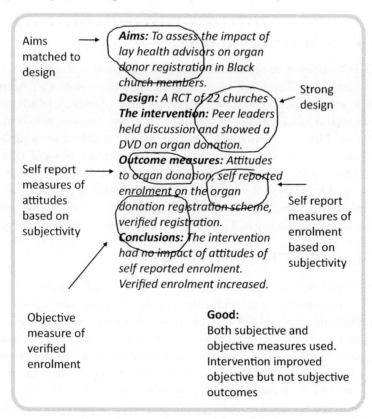

Aims matched to design

Aims: To assess the impact of lay health advisors on organ donor registration in Black church members.

Design: A RCT of 22 churches
The intervention: Peer leaders held discussion and showed a DVD on organ donation.

Strong design

Self report measures of attitudes based on subjectivity

Outcome measures: Attitudes to organ donation, self reported enrolment on the organ donation registration scheme, verified registration.

Conclusions: The intervention had no impact of attitudes of self reported enrolment. Verified enrolment increased.

Self report measures of enrolment based on subjectivity

Objective measure of verified enrolment

Good:
Both subjective and objective measures used. Intervention improved objective but not subjective outcomes

IS IT ALWAYS AS SIMPLE AS THAT?

Types of measurement, however, are not always as simple as a clear distinction between objective and subjective. All measures involve some level of researcher involvement whether it is in terms of choice of what to measure, how to measure it, or just taking the reading from a blood test or monitor, checking for cancer cells, or reading an x-ray or MRI scan, all of which are open to the subjectivity of the researcher. Therefore, even measures classified as objective are embedded with an element of subjectivity. Furthermore, those constructs, which are themselves subjective, such as beliefs, attitudes, or values can at times be measured in ways that are more objective. For example, whilst pain is subjective it could be measured in terms of self-administered pain medication; political views could be measured using voting behaviour, and prejudice could be measured in terms of shortlisting someone for an interview.

There are therefore multitudes of variables that can be measured in a multitude of ways. It is helpful to classify them as subjective or objective but this dichotomous classification should be seen as a guide not a rule.

THEORIES OF MEASUREMENT

In 1982, in his book 'Conceptualisation and Measurement in the Social Sciences' Blalock argued that 'The social sciences are facing serious problems'. According to Blalock, such problems have arisen out of the kinds of research which measure constructs such as social class, beliefs, emotions, behaviour, coping, well-being, and quality of life. How do researchers know that they are actually measuring beliefs? Are the measurements of coping accurate? Which measure of social class most closely relates to social class? To address these problems, a theory of measurement was developed involving a 2-stage process: conceptualisation and operationalisation. Furthermore, aspects of validity and reliability have developed to facilitate the effectiveness of these stages. This theory of measurement is shown in Figure 5.

STAGE 1: CONCEPTUALISATION

Blalock (1982) defined conceptualisation as 'a series of processes by which theoretical constructs, ideas, and concepts are clarified, distinguished, and given definitions that make it possible to reach a reasonable degree of consensus and understanding of the theoretical ideas we are trying to express'. Conceptualisation therefore involves the translation of a vague notion into a clearly bounded construct and is key to any attempt at measurement. It is also essential for communication as poorly conceptualised constructs can lead to confusion between research groups and create apparently contradictory

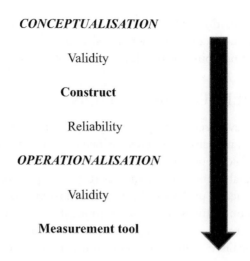

CONCEPTUALISATION

Validity

Construct

Reliability

OPERATIONALISATION

Validity

Measurement tool

Figure 5 Theories of measurement.

findings. For example, if a group of researchers were interested in the impact of cervical screening on health, their research conclusions could depend upon how their constructs were conceptualised. If health were conceptualised as 'the detection of abnormal cells' then a biomedical paper may conclude that cervical screening improved health status. In contrast, a psychology paper may conclude the reverse if health were conceptualised as 'anxiety and depression'. Likewise, if researchers wanted to measure the impact of a drug on depression they would need to conceptualise depression. This could be either as lowered mood (feeling sad, upset, miserable) or as a combination of mood and somatic symptoms such as loss of appetite, lowered libido, and poor sleep. How depression is conceptualised would then determine how it was measured and therefore whether or not the drug in question was shown to be effective.

The central role of conceptualisation is particularly apparent in the area of quality of life. Reports of a Medline search for the term 'quality of life' indicate a surge in its use over the past few decades. Researchers have therefore set about developing measures of quality of life but these have varied. For example, researchers have either focused on quality of life in the last year of life, quality of life in individuals with specific illnesses, quality of life from a health economics perspective, or with an emphasis on survival. They have also either focused on a single aspect of health such as mood or pain or a multidimensional perspective to capture the World Health Organisation's definition that states it is 'a broad ranging concept affected in a complex way by the person's physical health, psychological state, level of independence, social relationships, and their relationship to the salient features in their environment' (WHOQOL Group, 1993). Stage 1 of the theory of measurement therefore involves conceptualisation, which involves taking a vague notion and making it into a specific construct so that there is a shared language between researchers that is the starting point for the development of a measurement tool.

STAGE 2: OPERATIONALISATION

Once constructs have been conceptualised, stage 2 in the theory of measurement involves operationalisation. This has been defined by Bryman (1989) as 'the translation of concepts into observable entities' and reflects the development of an acceptable measure of the construct in question. For constructs such as 'patient', 'health professional', 'child', and so on this involves a process not dissimilar to conceptualisation. For example, if a study required the assessment of 'patient health', the concept 'patient' needs to be operationalised. It could be operationalised in many ways including 'person requiring treatment', 'person registered on a General Practice list', or more specifically 'person over the age of 16 attending their general practice in order to see the GP for their own health problem (not accompanying a child or other adult) within a year'. Such constructs therefore simply involve a clear definition and agreement between the researchers involved. Many researchers, however, are interested in more complex constructs that involve measurement tools such as interviews, semi-structured or structured questionnaires. These constructs also need to be operationalised as a means to develop ways of measuring them effectively. Accordingly, the definition of depression and anxiety is turned into a mood scale and the definition of quality of life is translated into a quality of life scale. For example, following the discussions concerning an acceptable definition of quality of life the European Organisation for Research on Treatment of Cancer operationalised quality of life in terms of 'functional status, cancer and treatment specific symptoms, psychological distress, social interaction, financial/economic impact, perceived health status, and overall quality of life' (Aaronson et al., 1993). Their measure then consisted of items to reflect these different dimensions. Likewise, the researchers who worked on the Rand Corporation health batteries operationalised quality of life in terms of 'physical functioning, social functioning, role limitations due to physical problems, role limitations due to emotional problems, mental health, energy/vitality, pain, and general health perception' which formed the basic dimensions of their scale (e.g. Stewart & Ware, 1992). Such tools are usually developed from items elicited from the literature, the researchers, and the subjects of the research or all three. The items are then organised into a questionnaire, which is piloted and finalised.

Many complex constructs are hard to measure. The theory of measurement and the two stages of conceptualisation and operationalisation provide a structure to ensure that an initial vague idea can be turned into a clear construct (stage 1) which in turn can be turned into an appropriate measurement tool (stage 2).

THE USEFULNESS OF ANY MEASUREMENT TOOL

Although the theory of measurement and the stages of conceptualisation and operationalisation clarify the process of developing a measurement tool, many questions remain about the usefulness of the final tool. These include: 'Are all items in the measure, measuring the same thing'?, 'Does the tool really measure the construct in question'?, 'How do researchers know that their constructs are being measured by their measurement tools'?, 'Has the construct been accurately operationalised'? To evaluate the usefulness of any measurement tool and to assess its accuracy researchers use aspects of reliability and validity.

Reliability is 'concerned with the consistency of a measure' (Bryman, 1989) and is relevant to both stages of conceptualisation and operationalisation. In essence, reliability questions whether the measure as a whole, and the individual items included in that measure, generate roughly similar results when assessed under roughly similar conditions. The most common forms of reliability are as follows:

Internal reliability: This assesses whether the items within a measure are suitably related to each other to justify adding them together and calling them a single variable. This is the most common form of reliability. For example, if depression is conceptualised as including both mood symptoms (feeling sad, miserable) and somatic symptoms (loss of appetite, poor sleep), then operationalised using items to measure each of these symptoms a reliable measurement tool would show that those who scored high on 'feeling sad' would also tend to score high on each of the other items being measured. This can be assessed using factor analysis or principal component analysis (in line with item response theory) followed by Cronbach's alpha.

Test–retest reliability: This refers to the consistency of a measure over time. To assess this the measure is completed by the same participants at two time points to assess how stable it is. It only makes sense to do this if it is predicted that a variable will be stable and a trait measure rather than changeable and a state measure.

Split half reliability: This assesses the consistency between the different halves of the same measure. To assess this the measure is split in half and each half given to the same participants to complete. This only works if both halves of the measure are conceptualised to be measuring the same construct.

Inter rater reliability: This assesses the degree of consistency between different raters of the same variables. It can be achieved through debate, collaboration, focus groups, and the Delphi method, which involves generating new ideas and commenting on each idea until agreement

49

is reached. It can also be achieved through explicitly comparing scores between raters and testing their similarity using tests such as the Kappa.

Intra rater reliability: This assesses the consistency within the same rater on the same variables but at different time points.

Unreliable measures include random variability, which means we cannot be sure that we know what we are measuring and what the results mean.

Validity refers to 'the issue of how we can be sure that a measure really does reflect the concept to which it is supposed to be referring' (Bryman, 1989). The most common forms of validity are as follows:

Face validity: This requires researchers to believe that a concept makes sense and that its definition reflects the construct itself. For example, if trying to measure depression, the researcher would scrutinise each item in the scale to check that it matches their conceptualisation of depression. There is no statistical test for face validity it is just a matter of scrutiny and consensus between researchers if more than one researcher is involved.

Sampling or content validity: This assesses whether the measure taps into all the dimensions that have been conceptualised as making up each given construct. Therefore, if quality of life is conceptualised as consisting of mood, pain, activity of daily living, and general health status then adequate content validity would mean that it contained items to measure these aspects of quality of life. This is also assessed just by scrutinising the measure.

Concurrent validity: Many constructs have existing definitions or measurement tools. Concurrent validity assesses the degree to which any one measure correlates with existing definitions of measures. This is assessed using a correlation coefficient. So if there exists a detailed clinical interview for diagnosing a mental health issue such as an Eating Disorder, a new self-report measure of an Eating Disorder would need to correlate with the scores from the clinical interview to show that it had concurrent validity.

Incremental validity: This assesses the extent to which a new measure is 'better' than existing measurement tools. In the area of health status, it is becoming clear that simple single items to measure health status such as 'How would you rate your health'? are as good, if not better than far more detailed and complex measures at predicting health outcomes including mortality. Therefore these would seem to have incremental validity.

The processes of reliability and validity are used to assess the success of the stages of conceptualisation and operationalisation. In particular, face validity, inter rater reliability and content validity are useful for conceptualisation to check that a construct has been clearly conceptualised and that researchers agree on a common language and meaning for their construct. In addition, the remaining types of reliability and validity help with the stage of operationalisation to test whether the measure is in some way measuring what it is supposed to measure.

FROM CONCEPTUALISATION TO OPERATIONALISATION: THE EXAMPLE OF HEALTH STATUS

This chapter has described the different types of measurement tools, the theory of measurement, and the stages of conceptualisation and operationalisation and how the usefulness of any tool can be evaluated using reliability and validity. This will now be illustrated in terms of health status and the different ways in which it has been measured. This is shown in Figure 6.

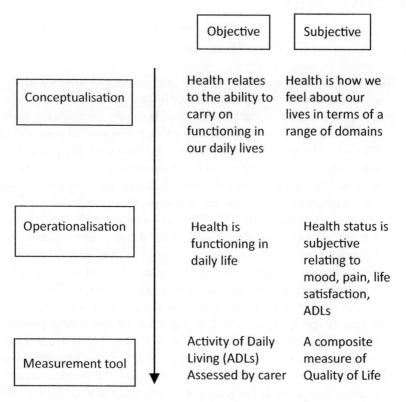

Figure 6 From conceptualisation to operationalisation: the example of health status.

The notion of 'health' can be conceptualised in a multitude of ways. It could simply be 'the absence of illness', or 'feeling well', or it could mean 'having a good quality of life' and for some it might mean 'not being dead'. As a result, it can also be operationalised through the production of measurement tools in ways as varied as a medical diagnosis, blood tests, simple self-report measures, complex self-report measures, and even the absence or presence of life. These different tools will now be considered and the ways they illustrate a different process of conceptualisation and operationalisation.

DIFFERENT MEASUREMENT TOOLS TO MEASURE HEALTH STATUS

Health status can be measured using both objective and subjective measurement tools

OBJECTIVE TOOLS

Objective tools are independent of the person being studied and so not open to response bias and social desirability factors.

> **Mortality rates:** If conceptualised as 'the presence or absence of life or death' the most basic measure of health status takes the form of a very crude mortality rate, which is calculated by simply counting the number of deaths in one year compared with either previous or subsequent years. This asks 'Has the number of people who have died this year gone up, gone down, or stayed the same'? and an increase in mortality rate can be seen as a decrease in health status. This approach, however, requires a denominator to reflect the size of the population being studied and a measure of who is at risk. This allows comparisons to be made between different populations: More people may die in a given year in London when compared with Bournemouth, but London is simply bigger. Mortality rates can be corrected for age and sex and can be produced to be either age specific, such as infant mortality rates, or illness specific, such as sudden death rates. As long as the population being studied is accurately specified, corrected, and specific, mortality rates provide an easily available and simple measure: Death is a good objective measure of health when health is conceptualised as the absence or presence of life.

> **Morbidity rates:** Mortality rates may seem like the perfect measure of health status for some, but researchers have now challenged this position to ask the seemingly obvious question, 'Is health really only the absence of

death'? This has resulted in a focus on morbidity that can also be assessed in a more objective way by simply counting how many people within a given population suffer from a particular problem using their medical records. Likewise, sickness absence rates simply count days lost due to illness and caseload assessments count the number of people who visit their general practitioner or hospital within a given time frame. Such morbidity rates provide details at the level of the population in general and reflect the conceptualisation of health as the 'presence of illness'. However, morbidity is also measured for each individual using measures of functioning.

Measures of functioning: Measures of functioning ask the question, 'To what extent can you do the following tasks'? and are generally called activity-of-daily-living scales (ADLs). These are often completed by the researcher or carer and involve observation and ratings of a number of activities such as bathing, dressing, continence, and feeding. If health is conceptualised as relating to functioning than the ADL is the operationalisation of this notion of health.

• •

SUBJECTIVE TOOLS

Mortality and morbidity rates and ADLs are mostly completed by a researcher or carer and aim to be objective as they avoid the experiences and views of the person being studied. In contrast, subjective measures make this experience and view their focus. They therefore reflect the conceptualisation of health status as a subjective state and operationalise it accordingly. Subjective measures of health status are either unidimensional or multidimensional and are always based on self-report.

Unidimensional measures: Some measures of health status focus on one aspect of health status such as mood, pain, self-esteem, or life satisfaction. To assess functioning from the perspective of the patient, ADLs have also been developed for individuals themselves to complete and include questions such as, 'Do you or would you have any difficulty: washing down/cutting toenails/running to catch a bus/going up/down stairs'? Therefore, if health status is conceptualised in a focused way it can be operationalised using a unidimensional measurement tool.

Multidimensional measures: Other measures of health status are multidimensional in that they take a more global approach to health status and assess health status in the broadest sense. Some of these are single item scales, some are composite scales, and some are individual quality of life scales: (i) **Single item scales:** Measuring health status does not have to be a long and complicated process and some scales use a

53

THINKING CRITICALLY ABOUT RESEARCH

single item such as, 'Would you say your health is: excellent/good/ fair/poor'?, 'Rate your current state of health' on a scale ranging from 'poor' to 'perfect' or from 'best possible' to 'worst possible'. Researchers have also developed single item self-report measures of fitness which ask 'would you say that for someone your own age your fitness is . . . ' with the response options being very good/good/moderate/poor/very poor. These simple scales have been shown to correlate highly with other more complex measures and to be useful as an outcome measure. They have also been shown to be good predictors of mortality. (ii) **Composite measures:** Because health status is often conceptualised in more complex ways involving a number of different domains, it is mostly operationalised using complex composite measures. Some focus on particular populations, such as the elderly or children while others focus on specific illnesses, such as diabetes or HIV. These composite measures may assess domains such as pain, mood, ADLs, and life satisfaction and are sometimes considered to assess quality of life. (iii) **Individual quality of life scales:** Although composite scales are subjective, the items in the scales are chosen by the researcher and may not reflect the patient's own priorities. Therefore, researchers have developed individual quality-of-life measures, which not only ask the subjects to rate their own health status but also to define the dimensions along which it should be rated. For example, if exercise, music, and friends are important dimensions then they will rate these domains. These more multidimensional measures of health status reflect a conceptualisation that is broad and encompasses a more complex notion of health.

Health status illustrates the ways in which 'health' can be conceptualised and how these different ways are operationalised to create different measurement tools. The usefulness of each of these tools can then be assessed using aspects of reliability and validity.

IN SUMMARY

Thinking critically about research involves an understanding of methodology and this chapter has focused on measurement. It has described the range of measurement tools that can be used and described the theory of measurement and the role of conceptualisation and operationalisation. It has also shown how the usefulness of a tool can be assessed using reliability and validity. Finally, it has used health status as an example to illustrate how these different processes come together. The next component to knowing methods is data analysis which is the focus of the next chapter.

5

KNOWING DATA ANALYSIS

● ●

OVERVIEW

All data is eventually analysed so the findings can be presented to the world. This involves a process of data reduction and data synthesis as it makes no sense to state 'here are my 120 participants and their 250 data points' and much more sense to classify and categorise this data in some way. For quantitative data, analysis involves statistics. For qualitative data, analysis involves the search for patterns, themes, or categories. Both involve the search for a story. This is not a data analysis book but critical thinking involves some understanding of data analysis. This chapter will therefore describe what data analysis can be done for both quantitative and qualitative approaches and how to make sense of the findings.

● ●

QUANTITATIVE DATA ANALYSIS

Statistics often frightens people who get lost and confused by the complexity of terms, numbers, computer printouts, and jargon. Thinking critically about quantitative analysis involves an understanding of what analysis can be done and what the findings mean.

WHAT QUANTITATIVE DATA ANALYSIS CAN BE DONE?

At its most basic there are only three ways to analyse quantitative data (i) **Describing it:** Data can be analysed by simply describing it using descriptive statistics. This can involve counting in terms of numbers and percentages or summated to find the average (whether it be the mean, mode, or median). Data which is not on a scale such as sex (male vs. female), health condition (cancer vs. diabetes), or exam results (pass vs. fail) is called nominal data and can be described as a count or percentage. Data on a scale with some sort of order (called ordinal data), such as social class (working/middle/upper), degree results (3rd / 2:2/ 2:1/ 1st) or body size (underweight/normal weight/overweight/obese) can be described using the median as the average. Data on a proper scale (called interval data) can be described using the mean as the average. Examples of interval data are height, weight, or age as the gaps between each item on the same are equal (i.e. intervals). Descriptive data analysis can be presented in many ways such as line graphs, pie charts, or histograms. (ii) **Looking for differences:** Data can also be analysed to look for differences between different variables. This requires there being one variable which has two categories such as sex (male vs. female); group (patient vs. Dr); health condition (Diabetes vs. not) or more than two categories such as intervention (drug vs. treatment as usual vs. placebo) or time (baseline vs. six months follow up vs. 12 months follow up). This is known as the grouping variable (also called condition/between subjects factor/within subject factor/fixed factor/arm of trial). If the groups are different people (i.e. male vs. female; drug vs. treatment as usual vs. placebo) then the analysis uses an independent groups analysis as the groups are independent of each other (also called between subjects). If the groups are the same people (i.e. baseline vs. 6 months vs. 12 months follow up) then the analysis uses a non–independent groups analysis (also called within subjects or paired or repeated measures). Examples of statistical tests used to look for differences are *t*-tests, ANOVAs, Chi–square, Mann Witney U, Kruskal Wallis, and Odds Ratios. Most analyses to look for differences can be drawn either on a bar chart (when one variable is a grouping variable and the other is on a scale of some sort) or in a two by two table (or two by three/three by three/fiveby five etc.) when neither variable is on a scale. (iii) **Looking for associations:** The third way data can be analysed is to look for associations. This usually involves two or more variables that are on some sort of scale to assess whether when one variable increases the other one also increases (or decreases). Associations between two variables are often drawn as a scatter plot with an X- and Y-axis with a line drawn between the data points. This assesses a correlation. A line going up indicates a positive correlation (as people get taller they also get heavier). A line going down indicates a negative correlation (as people get older they walk less quickly). A horizontal line indicates no association between the variables (Money is unrelated to happiness). In statistics, this generates a correlation coefficient with the sign of the coefficient indicating whether the correlation is positive or negative. Analysis can also explore the associations between many variables at once. Example of statistical tests that look for the association between two variables are Pearson's and Spearman's correlations. Examples of tests which look at more complex associations include linear regression, multiple regression, structural equation modelling, factor analysis, and cluster analysis.

All simple and complex data analyses tend to involve one of these three approaches: describing, looking for differences, or looking for associations. Have a look at Task 6 and decide which approach to data analysis is needed for the different research questions.

Task 6 What types of data analysis would you use?

Would the following research questions be answered using statistics to **describe** the data, to look for **differences** or to look for **associations**? (please circle)

Example	Types of data analysis?
Does increased exercise reduce depression?	Describe / differences / associations
How many young people smoke cigarettes?	Describe / differences / associations
Are older people more lonely than younger people?	Describe / differences / associations
Do condoms prevent the transmission of the AIDS virus?	Describe / differences / associations
Are people who do exercise less depressed than those who don't?	Describe / differences / associations
How much screen time to children watch each day?	Describe / differences / associations
How many people eat 5 fruit and veg per day?	Describe / differences / associations
Does good weather change our mood?	Describe / differences / associations
Are men more aggressive than women?	Describe / differences / associations
Do children who have ipads weight more than those who don't?	Describe / differences / associations
How do young people feel about vaping?	Describe / differences / associations
Does screen time cause obesity?	Describe / differences / associations
Does poor parenting lead to increased screen time?	Describe / differences / associations
Does loneliness lead to depression?	Describe / differences / associations
How many people practice safe sex?	Describe / differences / associations

HOW TO MAKE SENSE OF THE FINDINGS?

Quantitative data analysis produces statistics that need to be understood and interpreted. There are many very detailed books on statistics and this is beyond the remit of this book (see Field, 2018). But the basics of statistics are described as follows:

Descriptive data: Data is often described using measures of distribution such as the mean, median or mode, standard deviations, percentages, counts, and percentiles. These measures are useful to interpret the results and show the spread of data both between groups and within any given sample. On their own, they do not tell us how meaningful the findings are.

Statistical tests: Data can then be analysed using statistical tests to produce statistics such as the t (from t-tests), F (from ANOVAs), and X^2 (the chi square from cross tabs). These illustrate whether or not the differences or associations we find are likely to be meaningful. However, on their own they do not tell us whether they are meaningful.

The p-value: Statistical tests are often followed by the p-value (probability) which is an indicator of the significance of the finding. The p-value tests the likelihood that the findings you get from the analysis are more different or similar than they would be by chance. This is because most things are just different (men vs. women, old vs. young, ill vs. healthy). But we want to know whether this difference is meaningful and rather than just saying 'it's a big difference' or 'it's a small difference', we say it is a significant difference which means it is bigger than what we would expect by chance. The p-value is traditionally set at 0.05 and anything below this is considered to be significant (i.e. <0.05). This is a random cut off point that has been used for decades and means that 1/20 (i.e. 0.05/100) of tests will be significant by chance. The main problem with p-values is that if you 'fish' in your data and search for significance by carrying out multiple tests, by chance 1/20 of these tests will come out as significant.

Effect sizes: P-values tell us if any difference we find in our data is different to that predicted by chance. P-values do not tell us the size of the difference. Statistical tests are therefore also accompanied with a measure of effect size. The effect size can be a Cohen's d, partial eta squared, Relative Risk, Odds ratio, or correlation coefficient (r or R). Some research also uses the Number Needed to Treat (NNT). This is a specific calculation of how many people need to receive the intervention for one person to benefit (i.e. a NNT of two means that two people need to have the intervention for one person to benefit i.e. 50% chance of success). Researchers also use the NNH (Number Needed to Harm) which is similar to the NNT but a measure of harm. Therefore, an NNH of 10 means that for every 10 people who receive the intervention, one person will experience harm or an NNH of two means that there is a 50% chance of harm for any intervention. Sometimes the effect size is described as small, medium, or large. Large effect sizes are desirable if an intervention is costly, time consuming, or has potential side effects. Small effect sizes are more acceptable if the intervention has a much wider reach, is cheap, and has few side effects. We would therefore want a heart bypass operation to have a large effect size so that most people would benefit. But it would be more acceptable to have a small effect size for a billboard recommending that drivers take a break when tired as this would do little harm but a few people might benefit.

Confidence intervals: P-values therefore assess whether any difference we find is greater than chance and effect sizes tell us the size of this difference. Research often also uses Confidence Intervals (CIs) to overcome the problem with p-values. Rather than asking 'is a difference bigger than predicted by chance'? the confidence interval asks 'how confident can we be that the difference we found in our sample is similar to the difference in the population we want to generalise to'? The confidence interval is therefore a measure of the precision of the data we have and can be applied to any data (differences, associations, or just means) to show how precise or accurate our data is compared to the wider population. To do this, the analysis generates a range of data points around any variable in our data set to reflect the range of data that could be expected in the wider population. It therefore creates a virtual population. If we are comparing one variable between two groups it will generate a range around this variable for each group (i.e. in the wider population the data would fall within this range for each of the groups). If these ranges (the CIs) for each of the two groups overlap, we can conclude that in the wider population they would also overlap and are therefore not different. If they do not overlap then we can conclude that in the wider population they would not overlap and therefore are different. For example, if we want to know whether height differs between men and women, the computer generates a range (CI) around height for men and height for women and we can see if these ranges (CIs) overlap. If they overlap they are not different, if they do not overlap they are different. We can therefore have a sense of how confident we are that in the wider population there would or would not be a difference of the size we have found in our data. CIs are also generated around the difference between two groups. If this doesn't cross zero (i.e. both positive or both negative) then this also means that the difference is 'significant'.

Quantitative data analysis therefore asks questions of the data and produces statistical results that can be interpreted using p-values, effects sizes, and CIs. These different statistical tests are illustrated in Worked Example 7.

Worked Example 7 Using statistics.

CRASH2: a RCT of Tranexamic acid (TXA) to prevent death in trauma patients (Roberts et al., 2013).

Aims: *to assess the impact of TXA on death in trauma patients*
Design: *Randomised placebo controlled trial*
Sample: *20211 adult patients within 8 hours of trauma with or at risk of significant bleeding*
Results: *All-cause mortality at 28 days was significantly reduced by TXA [1463 patients (14.5%) in the TXA group vs 1613 patients (16.0%) in the placebo group; relative risk (RR) 0.91; 95% confidence interval (CI) 0.85 to 0.97; p = 0.0035]. The risk of death due to bleeding was significantly reduced [489 patients (4.9%) died in the TXA group vs 574 patients (5.7%) in the placebo group; RR 0.85; 95% CI 0.76 to 0.96; p = 0.0077].*
Conclusion: *TXA reduces death in trauma patients if given within 3 hours.*

Descriptive statistics of difference

Calculate NNT: 1.5% difference (ie 1.5/100) NNT=66

Relative risk – measure of effect size

95% CIs: estimation of difference in wider population. Do not cross zero.

P value: assessment of significance against chance. Usual cut off is p<0.05

. . . .

QUALITATIVE DATA ANALYSIS

Qualitative methods such as interviews and focus groups are useful to ask exploratory questions and can generate novel and rich data. Thinking critically about qualitative data analysis involves an understanding of what data analysis can be done.

WHAT QUALITATIVE DATA ANALYSIS CAN BE DONE?

There are many different types of qualitative analysis such as conversational analysis (CA), discourse analysis (DA), thematic analysis (TA), grounded theory analysis (GTA), Interpretative Phenomenological Analysis (IPA), and narrative analysis (NA). Qualitative analysis can also involve data from a range of sources including interviews and focus groups, drawings, photographs, advertisements, clothing, TV programmes, and clinical consultations some of which may have been generated specifically for a study but some may be independent of research and more naturally occurring. Here is not the place to describe each and to attempt to outline their similarities and differences. But in essence, I think qualitative data analysis can do one of three things: (i) **Describe the data:** Some approaches to qualitative analysis emphasise describing how or what their participants feel or think or what the data in front of them shows. This involves findings patterns (themes, categories, ideas) in the data and pulling this together to reflect the overall story. From this perspective, the researcher is relatively passive, comes from an atheoretical position with no a priori models, theories, or expectations and does justice to the data. This is more of a classification approach. (ii) **Interpret the data:** Some researchers argue that it is unlikely that anyone comes to their data with no preconceptions, as we are all human beings with life experiences, beliefs, and feelings of our own. From this perspective, qualitative data analysis is therefore seen to involve the interpretation, rather than simple description of the data. In line with this, researchers may generate a pattern from the data (themes, categories, ideas) but acknowledge and even emphasise the ways in which they are drawing upon who they are, to interpret what their participants have said or what the data is showing. From this perspective, qualitative data analysis is about interpretation and the analysis emerges from an interaction between the researcher and their data. (iii) **Analyse what the data is doing:** From a different perspective some qualitative data analysis emphasises what the data is doing rather than how it reflects what people think or feel. From this perspective, data (i.e. words, images etc.) are seen as active and functional and sometimes called 'text acts'. Therefore, if someone uses the phrase 'I feel sad' in an interview, rather than analysing this as illustrating their underlying mood (as in describing or interpreting the data) this would be seen as a form of communication or expression which is designed to persuade others to see them as being sad (not that they are actually sad). Accordingly, qualitative data analysis sometimes sees data as having a function and then analyses what this function might be. An example of qualitative analysis is illustrated in Worked Example 8.

Worked Example 8 Qualitative analysis.

The experience of leg ulcers (Tollow & Ogden, 2017).

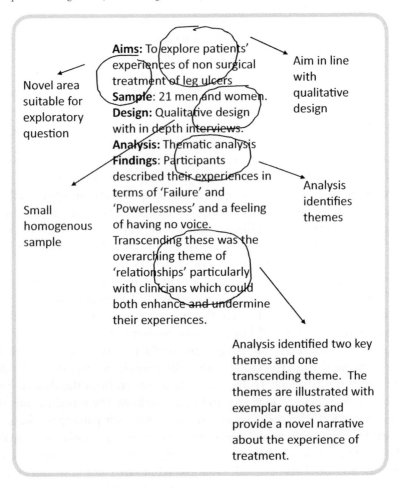

Novel area suitable for exploratory question

Aims: To explore patients' experiences of non surgical treatment of leg ulcers

Aim in line with qualitative design

Sample: 21 men and women.
Design: Qualitative design with in depth interviews.
Analysis: Thematic analysis
Findings: Participants described their experiences in terms of 'Failure' and 'Powerlessness' and a feeling of having no voice. Transcending these was the overarching theme of 'relationships' particularly with clinicians which could both enhance and undermine their experiences.

Small homogenous sample

Analysis identifies themes

Analysis identified two key themes and one transcending theme. The themes are illustrated with exemplar quotes and provide a novel narrative about the experience of treatment.

IN SUMMARY

Thinking critically about research involves an understanding of research methods. So far, this section has explored knowing the basic features of research, design, and measurement. This chapter has focused on data analysis in terms of both quantitative data analysis with its focus on number and statistics and qualitative data analysis with its focus on patterns, themes, and narratives. The next step involves thinking critically about all these aspects of the research process.

WHAT IS CRITICAL THINKING AND HOW TO DO IT?

Thinking critically involves questioning whatever you are told. Thinking critically about research involves asking questions such as 'Are the researchers allowed to say that'?, 'does that match with what they have done'?, 'what would need to be done to know that'?, 'is it possible to know that'?, and 'are those conclusions justified'? I don't think people should become mindlessly skeptical of everything they read as it becomes tedious to hear someone shout 'rubbish' at everything. This isn't critical thinking. But neither should people believe everything and be gullible just because they have read it in an academic journal or seen it reported in the press. So critical thinking is somewhere between skepticism and being gullible. This way you are not a bore but neither are you taken in by bad research. I have illustrated this in Figure 7.

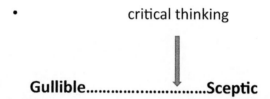

Figure 7 The ideal end result.

Thinking critically about research involves questioning 'what evidence is there' and 'how is that evidence presented'?

The next section outlines a wide range of problems and issues that you need to be aware of when thinking critically about research and focuses on:

WHAT EVIDENCE IS THERE?

STEP 2

THINKING CRITICALLY ABOUT METHOD

WHAT EVIDENCE IS THERE?

STEP 2

THINKING CRITICALLY ABOUT METHOD
WHAT EVIDENCE IS THERE?

6
THINKING CRITICALLY ABOUT THE BASICS

• •

OVERVIEW

Thinking critically about research involves being aware of the potential problems and pitfalls associated with different aspects of methodology. Chapter 2 described the basic features common across all research studies. This chapter focuses on identifying a research area, the sample and the final story, and highlights some of the key problems with these basic features such as researcher bias, response bias, representativeness, generalisability, and whether a study passes the 'so what'? test. Key problems are illustrated with worked examples from published research papers.

• •

IDENTIFYING A RESEARCH AREA

Choosing a research area involves synthesising existing research to identify a gap. This can involve a narrative review, systematic review, or meta-analysis. These processes have three problems.

Researcher bias: A narrative analysis purports to be a review of the existing research in order to identify a gap in the literature and set the scene for the subsequent study. Researcher bias is a particular problem for a narrative analysis as the researcher decides which papers to select and how to pull them together to create a coherent story that establishes their study as the perfect way to fill the gap that they have identified. In fact, often the literature is reviewed after the study has been completed and the results are known. This means that a narrative review does not constitute either a review of all the relevant research or an objective analysis of this literature but a subjective analysis that fits the study being done. This is central to the creative process of being a researcher but it also introduces an element of researcher bias as the researcher's own beliefs, perspectives, and motivations will influence the direction of the review. The solution to the problems inherent with a narrative review is a systematic review that details the search terms and search engines used so that the process can be replicated by an independent other. This is still, however, embedded with researcher bias as even if the papers selected are the same, two (or more) researchers may well come up with their own conclusions following their own version of the synthesis process. Many systematic reviews also have another problem, that of apples and pears.

Apples and pears: Systematic reviews were introduced to answer very specific research questions and to synthesise papers that address the same question using similar designs and similar samples. Sometimes, however, this method is used to synthesise studies that ask different questions, use different designs, and have different samples. This is the problem of apples and pears and is problematic as variability in the findings of the different studies may just be due to the variability in the studies themselves. A conclusion that a 'final' answer to the specific research question is now known is therefore flawed as the problem of apples and pears means that researchers are not synthesising like with like. This is why many systematic reviews conclude 'more research is needed' and are therefore premature.

Premature reviews: Both systematic reviews and meta-analyses require similar studies with similar designs and samples. Although initial searches can lead to thousands of potential papers, the majority are often excluded, as most don't meet the stringent inclusion criteria. This can result in a small handful of papers to review. This is far more practical than trying to synthesise hundreds of papers but often means that the synthesis is premature and the conclusion is 'more research is needed'. If more papers are included then the conclusion is sometimes 'existing research is of poor quality. More research of better quality is needed'.

● ●

THE SAMPLE

The sample in any study determines whom the findings are relevant for and limits any conclusions that can be drawn. There are several problems with samples in most research studies. The problem of sampling is illustrated in Worked Example 9.

Not representative: The sample in any quantitative study is supposed to reflect and be representative of a wider population. To achieve this, researchers should employ a sampling method to sample randomly or in a stratified way. Many studies do not do this but take an opportunistic or convenience sample of whom they can get. Therefore, psychology studies use psychology students, market researchers use those who

Worked Example 9 Is the sample representative?

The impact of birth order on personality (Healey & Ellis, 2007).

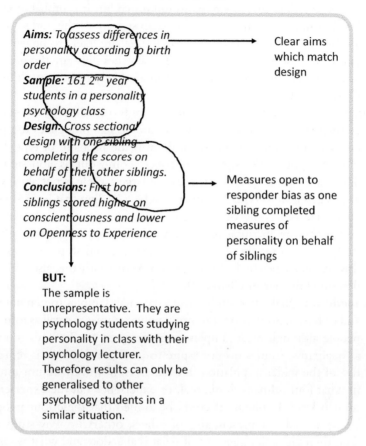

Aims: *To assess differences in personality according to birth order*

Clear aims which match design

Sample: *161 2nd year students in a personality psychology class*

Design: *Cross sectional design with one sibling completing the scores on behalf of their other siblings.*

Conclusions: *First born siblings scored higher on conscientiousness and lower on Openness to Experience*

Measures open to responder bias as one sibling completed measures of personality on behalf of siblings

BUT:
The sample is unrepresentative. They are psychology students studying personality in class with their psychology lecturer. Therefore results can only be generalised to other psychology students in a similar situation.

are happy to be stopped in the street, open their doors, or answer their telephones and medical researchers use those who go to their doctor (rather than suffer at home) and all researchers use those participants who consent to take part in the study.

Response bias: When describing a sample, researchers should give the response rate to show how many people they approached, how many people consented, and how many people completed the different stages of the study. This gives some idea of the representativeness of the sample. Many studies, however, do not do this. Recently researchers have started to use online surveys to collect data through platforms such as Twitter or Facebook. There is no way that anyone knows the denominator for such studies and how many people saw the link and declined to open it and take part. Likewise, there is now a data gathering system called Mechanical Turk whereby people in the US register and are paid for each online study they take part in. Again, the denominator remains unknown but it is probably millions. Furthermore, the kinds of people who sign up to this and sit at home all day doing surveys for very little money are likely to be very different to the rest of the population. These issues illustrate the problem of response bias and those who respond are likely to be very different to those who do not.

Under/overpowered: When samples are too small, they are said to be underpowered. This is because the sample size influences the p-value and when a sample is too small there is the problem of type 1 errors whereby potentially significant effects come out as non-significant. These are false negatives. However, a large sample is not always better as this can lead to type 2 errors whereby a finding that has a very small effect size can come out as significant (false positives). To solve this, researchers are encouraged to carry out a power calculation before the study starts to set the necessary sample size and stop recruiting once this has been reached. There are problems with this also, which are described further in Chapter 9.

Anecdotal: Qualitative studies use very small samples to generate novel and rich data. Sometimes this can involve samples as small as four or five people although most samples range between 10–20. This is justified, as qualitative studies do not aspire to generate data that is representative of the wider population. Researchers, however, are not interested in what four humans think, feel, or experience but the experiences of human kind. Implicitly it could be argued that these four people are being treated as representative of others, otherwise why study them? This then raises the question of what is anecdote and what is research? When I state in a lecture that 'my friend said . . . '; this is anecdote. But if I conclude from my study that 10 people said xxx is this anecdote or research? Some qualitative researchers solve this problem by collecting new data until they have reached saturation and no new ideas emerge. The small sample size is therefore justified as they have accessed all the possible thoughts/feelings/experiences on the topic. My solution to this problem is to accept that qualitative data is not representative but to believe that anecdote, and several people's anecdotes, together with novels, films, and poetry all have something useful to tell us about the human condition.

Not generalisable: As a result of the sampling issues outlined earlier, most studies are limited in the generalisability of their findings to other people other than those in the study. Some can be generalised to other people very similar to those in the study but all results should be interpreted with caution and seen within the confines of who was approached for the study, who agreed to take part, and who ultimately took part.

• •

THE FINAL STORY

The final story describes how the findings add to the existing literature. This can be evaluated in terms of two questions:

So what? Disciplines create their own sets of research questions and their own frameworks for deciding what should and should not be studied. Once completed, research studies are then written up using the language and format of each discipline, published by journals edited by editors from within the same discipline, and read by fellow academics embedded within the same language and framework. This can lead to great in-depth research answering interesting questions aligned to theory and with the appropriate methodology. It can also lead to the 'science of the bleeding obvious' mystified by language and dressed up as more than it is. So when thinking critically about research it is useful to ask the 'so what' question, demystify the findings of any study by putting it into everyday language (imagine you are telling a friend in one brief sentence), and question whether you really needed to know this.

Was it worth it? It is also useful to ask 'was it worth it'? Research is done for many reasons: to teach students how to do research; to pass a formal qualification such as a certificate or degree; to answer an interesting question; for job satisfaction; to publish academic papers; for recognition by colleagues; for promotion; to keep your job as an academic and not be sacked; to bring in money to your institution; and to promote the reputation of your institution. All of these are worthwhile endeavours and can produce research studies of all levels of quality and usefulness that may be read or simply ignored. From this perspective, all research is worth it as it has been completed to achieve one of these goals. Research, however, can also be considered worth it (or not) according to the following criteria: (i) **Cost:** Researchers very rarely benefit financially from doing research. All research grants go to the institution and although they may pay salaries these are set within standardised scales for equity between researchers. But research still costs money and when this is public money it is useful to ask whether this money was well spent. This can be helped by evaluating the study in terms of its impact and reach; (ii) **Impact:** Some research takes place in laboratories and can take decades before it has any direct impact upon the world. Other research is more at the translational end of the continuum and can have a more direct impact upon the world. Impact can take many forms such as the generation of new knowledge, improved education, improved health, a better society, or a better informed public; (iii) **Reach:** Research can also be judged in terms of its reach and the numbers and geographical spread of those who benefit. For example, a small-scale study might only impact upon a small local community whereas another study might have implications for people worldwide.

Evaluating 'was it worth it'? therefore involves an assessment why the research was done together with an understanding of cost, impact, and reach. This process is not, however, as straightforward as it might seem as it is quite feasible for a small-scale study to be cheap, have a very local reach, but make a huge difference to the lives of a few (e.g. encouraging people to sing at the local old people's home). Or a study might cost a lot, have a huge reach, but make very little difference to the lives of the people it touches (e.g. educating people across the world about healthy eating). Or a study might be cheap, with a huge reach, but have a very small impact on many, but at least have some impact on a few (e.g. billboard campaigns to take a break when driving). Or a study might have been a learning process for someone who did a better study next time round. Balancing the different dimensions of why a study was done, cost, impact, and reach forms part of a cost effectiveness evaluation or a costs and consequences assessment. Yet trying to put a value on research, assessing the real cost, balancing this with real impact and reach is problematic and involves assessing all these dimensions, which comes with all the flaws identified in this book.

IN SUMMARY

Thinking critically involves being aware of the potential problems associated with the basics of any research study. The process of identifying a research area involves some degree of research synthesis, which may not always be as straightforward as it is presented, involving issues of researcher bias, trying to synthesise apples and pears, or when insufficient research has been carried out. There may also be problems with the sample that can limit the generalisability of the study due to issues of representativeness, response bias, power, and anecdote. These all limit any conclusions that can be made. Finally, these conclusions and the story they tell can also be critically analysed by asking 'so what'? and 'was it worth it' to assess the value of the study.

7

THINKING CRITICALLY ABOUT DESIGN

• •

OVERVIEW

The chosen research design frames the study, addresses the research question, and limits any conclusions that can be made. Chapter 3 described the main types of research design ranging from qualitative designs with interviews and focus groups to experiments and randomised control trials. This chapter will highlight the problems arising from the different research designs with a focus on researcher bias, reverse causality, the third factor problem, and ecological validity. It will also describe how these problems can be solved but how many of these solutions introduce their own problems. These different problems are illustrated with a worked example from a research study.

• •

RESEARCHER BIAS

The problem of researcher bias arises when the researcher's own values, beliefs, and expectations influence the course of the research study which in turn impacts upon the findings. The objectivity of the method is therefore contaminated by the subjectivity of the researcher. There are several design factors that may exacerbate the problem of researcher bias. Some of these problems are illustrated in Worked Example 10.

> **Quantitative studies:** Quantitative studies are considered to be more objective than qualitative studies and therefore less likely to be contaminated by researcher bias as their measures include numbers (which are less open to interpretation) and the data can be analysed using statistics (rather than sense-making by the researcher). The views of the researcher however, influence many stages of the research study including which study to do, which measures to include, what types of statistics to carry out, which analyses to report, and which story to tell. Each of these stages is key to the creative process of being a researcher. But it is also open to researcher bias.

Worked Example 10 The problem of researcher bias.

The rise and fall of rosiglitazone (an analysis by Nissen, 2010).

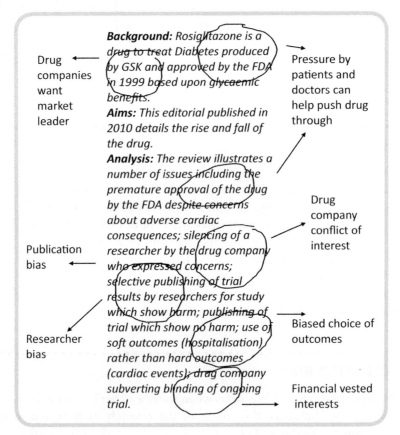

Drug companies want market leader

Background: *Rosiglitazone is a drug to treat Diabetes produced by GSK and approved by the FDA in 1999 based upon glycaemic benefits.*
Aims: *This editorial published in 2010 details the rise and fall of the drug.*
Analysis: *The review illustrates a number of issues including the premature approval of the drug by the FDA despite concerns about adverse cardiac consequences; silencing of a researcher by the drug company who expressed concerns; selective publishing of trial results by researchers for study which show harm; publishing of trial which show no harm; use of soft outcomes (hospitalisation) rather than hard outcomes (cardiac events); drug company subverting blinding of ongoing trial.*

Pressure by patients and doctors can help push drug through

Drug company conflict of interest

Publication bias

Researcher bias

Biased choice of outcomes

Financial vested interests

Qualitative studies: Essentially researcher bias is at the core of qualitative research as the researcher not only choses the research area and research question but also makes sense of the data and finds the story. This is what qualitative research is and this is an acceptable methodology as long as any conclusions made are in line with this design. Some researchers, however, have pushed to make qualitative research seem more objective and less biased by proposing checks and balances such as inter rater reliability (between two researchers), group analysis (between several researchers), creating a detailed paper trail of coding (for transparency so that someone else can agree or disagree with the codes), and generating a detailed step-by-step guide for how to analyse qualitative data so that any two people would follow the same path (and presumably identify the same patterns). This has resulted in a very prescriptive approach to qualitative methods and reflects the need to 'compete' with quantitative methods to make it more objective. There are several key problems with this new trajectory. First, it is not possible to make qualitative methods more objective as human beings carry out the analysis and even if two, three, or 20 people do the analysis they will each draw upon their own experiences and see something different. Second, it is not desirable to make qualitative methods more objective. Subjectivity is what this methodology is about and this should be celebrated. Third, trying to make qualitative methods more objective won't work but it might damage creativity which is central to this methodological approach. So, in essence, identifying subjectivity and researcher bias in quantitative methods is fine as they purport to be objective. But pointing the finger at qualitative methods in this way is meaningless as this is what they are.

Conflict of interest: Much researcher bias is implicit and works at a unconscious level. Some researchers, however, may be motivated by a more conscious form of bias due to a conflict of interest (COI). Conflict of interest is usually defined by academic journals in terms of financial gain and funding from drug companies, the food industry, or the tobacco industry, which can result in researchers having vested interests in their results coming out in a particular direction. This can lead to selective choices in terms of data collection and data analysis or it might even lead to outright fraud when results are fixed. Many conflicts of interest, however, are more subtle than this and often go undeclared. For example, a researcher carrying out a systematic review or meta-analysis of studies evaluating the impact of their own intervention, including their own research studies and/or their own theories will be biased towards showing a positive result (even if they have no financial gains to make). Likewise, a researcher from a particular discipline (e.g. psychology, biology, genetics) may be unconsciously motivated to show that their discipline provides a better explanation of the problem being considered than the other disciplines as this is the discipline they are most aligned with. Similarly, even a researcher with their own health condition (cancer, heart disease, pain, eating disorder, obesity, fatigue) may be motivated to show that this condition 'needs more research', 'causes much upset', 'is not the fault of the patient', or even 'can be treated effectively' due to their own personal experiences.

Expectations: One of the most powerful unconscious forms of researcher bias comes from expectations, and in the same way that a participant's expectations can influence outcomes (through the placebo effect) so can researcher expectations. For quantitative research, the mechanisms are not properly understood, but it is clear that by knowing which patient is in which arm of the trial or by expecting certain participants to show a particular response because of their known history, researchers can 'make this happen' which changes the results.

Solutions: Researcher bias is therefore a problem for all research studies and thinking critically about research involves recognising the potential impact of researcher bias on the findings and any conclusions drawn. Solutions to researcher bias include simply describing possible sources of bias in the research paper so at least this is transparent. This can take the form of a detailed COI statement (beyond just funding), a reflexivity statement in the methodology (to describe views/beliefs etc.), or a brief biography at the end of the paper (to describe disciplinary loyalties etc.). Researcher bias can also be minimised by the use of third party raters for a systematic review or meta-analysis, the use of an independent statistician to carry out the analysis, or blinding of the researcher as to the aims of the study or which participant is in which arm of a trial.

REVERSE CAUSALITY

Much research asks causal questions which are reflected not only in the term 'causes' but also 'predicts', 'impact upon', 'changes', 'affects', 'effects', and 'as a consequence'. The issue of causality arises when researchers ask a causal question but use an inappropriate research design. The main problem with attempting to make causal conclusions is that of reverse causality; although the conclusion may be 'A causes B' it is quite possible that 'B causes A'. The problem of reverse causality is illustrated in Figure 8. The problem of reverse causality arises from a number of different research designs.

Qualitative studies: Qualitative studies ask participants to describe their experiences and in answer they might say: 'I felt ill because I had done too much exercise' or 'I ate more because I was under stress'. But neither of these examples can be used to make causal conclusions. The design means that the findings illustrate what people think causes them to become ill or eat too much, not what really does. It could be that feeling ill makes them believe that they had done a lot of exercise, or eating too much makes them believe that they must have been stressed (reverse causality). Or this could just be their way of making sense of their lives when in fact these two factors are unrelated.

Cross-sectional design/case control studies: Studies that measure both variables independently but at the same time (i.e. How much exercise do you do? How is your health?) still cannot make claims about causality and again raise the problem of reverse causality. Even if one of the variables is framed in the past (e.g. 'how much exercise have you

'Being overweight is caused by doing less exercise'

OR

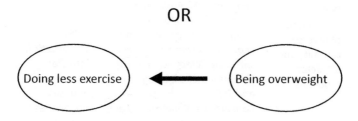

'People who are overweight do less exercise because they are overweight and feel embarrassed'

Always ask 'what else could be causing these findings'

Figure 8 The problem of reverse causality.

done'?, 'how is your health now'?) there remains the problem of reverse causality as it is quite possible that their current health status changes what they remember about their past exercise behaviour. The only time when cross-sectional designs can tentatively claim that reverse causality is not a problem is when one of the variables being measured is clearly and objectively in the past and not influenced by recall bias. For example, if a study asked 'how many siblings do you have'? and 'how many times have you been arrested' it is unlikely that being arrested lots of times has caused someone to have multiple siblings. However, it may well be that these two variables are just unrelated.

Longitudinal designs: Studies with baseline and follow up measures address the problem of reverse causality, as things in the future cannot cause things in the past. Therefore, if we measure exercise in January and depression the following June it cannot be said that depression caused the exercise. But because we tend to be creatures of habit and very consistent, it is quite likely that exercise in January was very similar to exercise in June and that the baseline measure of exercise was just

Worked Example 11 The problem of reverse causality.

Eating behaviour and health (Burkert, Muckenhuber, Großschädl, Rásky, & Freidl, 2014).

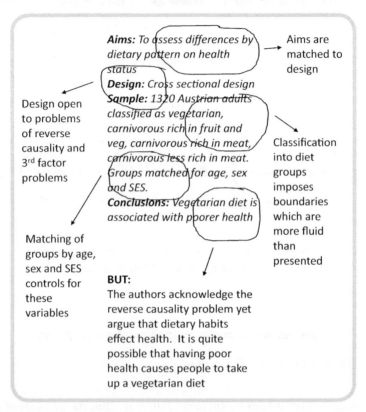

Design open
to problems
of reverse
causality and
3rd factor
problems

Aims: To assess differences by dietary pattern on health status

Design: Cross sectional design

Sample: 1320 Austrian adults classified as vegetarian, carnivorous rich in fruit and veg, carnivorous rich in meat, carnivorous less rich in meat. Groups matched for age, sex and SES.

Conclusions: Vegetarian diet is associated with poorer health

Aims are
matched to
design

Classification
into diet
groups
imposes
boundaries
which are
more fluid
than
presented

Matching of
groups by age,
sex and SES
controls for
these
variables

BUT:
The authors acknowledge the
reverse causality problem yet
argue that dietary habits
effect health. It is quite
possible that having poor
health causes people to take
up a vegetarian diet

a marker for follow up exercise. Longitudinal designs in part solve the problem of reverse causality, but causal conclusions still cannot be made. The problem of reverse causality is illustrated in Worked Example 11.

Solutions: Causality is core to many research questions yet causal conclusions cannot be drawn from qualitative, cross-sectional, or longitudinal designs due to the problem of reverse causality. The main solution to the problem of reverse causality is to use an experimental design due to the manipulation of the independent variable (the intervention) and the separation by time from the intervention to the follow up measure of the outcome variable. This design therefore solves the problem of reverse causality as any changes in the outcome variable cannot have caused the allocation to the specific arm of the intervention. For example, if people who receive exercise feel less depressed by follow up, it cannot be said that feeling less depressed made them be allocated to the exercise condition! Experimental designs therefore enable the strongest case to be made for causality. There still remains the third factor problem.

THE THIRD FACTOR PROBLEM

Research is often concerned with exploring the association between two or more variables and whether or not this association is considered to be causal. We may want to know whether exercise is related to feeling less depressed; education is related to financial success; whether diet is related to health; or whether parenting predicts happiness as an adult. The problem with making such associations is that although two variables may look like they are linked with each other, there may be many alternative explanations for this association. These are known as third factors, confounding variables, or sometimes spurious variables. For example, the reason why people who exercise are less depressed may be because they have more friends (to do exercise with). The friendships are what are important. Further, the reason educated people earn more, may be that they come from richer families who fund them through education for longer then put them into the family business with a higher salary. A rich family is the main factor linked to financial success not education. Likewise, the reason why diet is linked to health might be that those who eat a healthier diet also do exercise and don't smoke and come from a higher social class with more money and better living conditions. Diet is not the only factor explaining this association. Similarly, good parenting might predict happiness because 'good parents' have more time to spend with their children, because they have more money and don't have to work such long hours. Money and time are the real explanations not just good parenting. The third factor problem is illustrated in Figure 9.

> **Solutions:** The solution to the third factor problem is to rule out these alternative explanations by controlling for them. The method for doing this depends upon whether or not they have been measured: (i) **Controlling for them in the data analysis:** If the study has measured possible third factor variables then they can be controlled for in the analysis. This can be done either by 'taking them out of the analysis', using covariates, or 'putting them into the analysis' as additional predictor variables. The analysis then shows either that 'the link between exercise and depression still exists even when age, medication, gender, smoking, social class, and number of friends have been controlled for' or that 'the link between drinking red wine and longevity is actually due to having a good diet. Red wine has nothing to do with it'. (ii) **Controlling for them in the sampling:** Potential third factor variables can also be controlled for in the sampling method using a matching process. This is the key to case control designs and involves finding the target group (i.e. those with depression) and then matching them to a comparison group on all the variables that are predicted

'Drinking red wine makes you live longer'

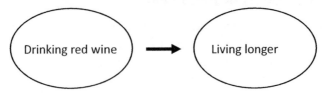

Possible 3rd factors

Smoking
Social class
Exercise
Where you live
Who you live with
OR
People who don't drink at all used to be alcoholics
or have another illness

Always ask *'what else could be causing these findings'*

Figure 9 The third factor problem.

not to cause depression. This rules out all of these matched variables as third factors as they are the same in both groups. The problem with this approach is knowing what to match for and potentially ruling out a key predictor of depression by using it as a matching variable. Both this matching approach and using statistics also require all potential third factors to be measured so that they can be controlled for. It is not possible to ever measure all third factors. (iii) **Using randomisation:** By far the best method to rule out third factors is to randomise participants to different groups. This means that the different groups should turn out matched without having to measure every possible variable. Therefore, not only will they be matched on obvious variables such as age, sex, smoking behaviour, and diet they will also be matched on whether they own a dog and like cartoons! The effectiveness of randomisation improves as the sample gets larger; if there are only 20 participants it is unlikely that they will come out even (just by chance). The third factor problem is illustrated in Worked Example 12.

Worked Example 12 The 3rd factor problem.

Exercise and the prevention of depression (Harvey et al., 2018).

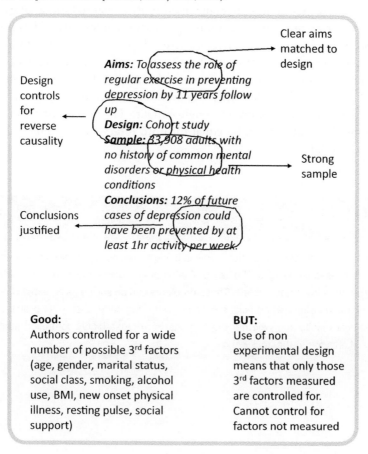

Good:

Authors controlled for a wide number of possible 3rd factors (age, gender, marital status, social class, smoking, alcohol use, BMI, new onset physical illness, resting pulse, social support)

BUT:

Use of non experimental design means that only those 3rd factors measured are controlled for. Cannot control for factors not measured

ECOLOGICAL VALIDITY

Researcher bias can be solved by distancing the researcher from the study and using methods of data collection (i.e. blinding) and data analysis (third party) that minimise the risk of interferences by the researcher. The problem of causality can be solved by experimental designs and the third factor problem can be best ruled out by randomisation. This leads to the conclusion that if we want to ask causal questions, and make sure that our conclusions are justified, the experiment (or RCT) is the gold standard design. Studies using these designs, however, come with their own problem: ecological validity. Creating a controlled and objective environment to carry out a study may make the conclusions more justified but this approach also raises the question 'are they also justified in the "real world" outside of the study'? This is known as eco-logical validity and relates to the criticism that some experimental studies are so artificial that they cannot be generalised to more naturalistic settings where variables interact, are complex, and people respond differently and more natu-rally. For example, in eating behaviour research, we often measure food intake in the laboratory in a controlled environment when the person is devoid of all food cues as a means to assess how much they eat. It could be argued that this lacks ecological validity. In an experimental design, all participants are measured in the same controlled environment. This means that the impact of ecological validity would be equal for both interventions. This makes the study more valid.

IN SUMMARY

Thinking critically about research involves being aware of the problems inherent in different research designs. The key problems are researcher bias, reverse causal-ity, and the third factor problem. These problems can be solved using experimental designs and controlled artificial settings which bring about their own problem of ecological validity and whether the findings from these highly controlled studies are still relevant to the 'real world'.

8

THINKING
CRITICALLY ABOUT
MEASUREMENT

OVERVIEW

The measures we use in any research study reflect the research question being asked and how this links to the existing literature. They also determine the conclusions that can be drawn from the findings. For some disciplines, measurement is more straightforward if the cells, gases, mass, or number can simply be counted. But for most disciplines (and even for these at times) the measurement process is problematic. Chapter 4 described the processes involved in measurement and the development of a measurement tool. This chapter describes how to think critically about measurement with a focus on problems such as not measuring what is supposed to be measured, subjectivity and bias, contamination by measurement, and reification.

NOT MEASURING WHAT IS SUPPOSED
TO BE MEASURED

One key problem with measurement is that the selected measure may not actually measure what it is supposed to be measuring. For example, I remember a psychology study supposedly about war and conflict, which operationalised conflict using a hypothetical vignette describing a football match. Measures were then taken of how participants would feel playing football against a hypothetical team. The conclusions were then about war and conflict. The researchers hadn't measured anything to do with war and conflict and so had measured the wrong thing. This problem can arise for a number of reasons:

Poor conceptualisation: Students are often told to define their terms for any essay. Researchers should do the same for their constructs but this is often not the case. The initial stage of conceptualisation is therefore often missing and the construct being measured remains poorly conceptualised. This is particularly the case for ambiguous constructs such as behaviour, emotions, attitudes, beliefs, and values. For example, prejudice could be an emotion ('I hate women') or a cognition ('women are less able then men').

It could be specific to one person ('My wife is useless') or concerned with a group of people ('all women are useless'). It could be a more observable behaviour ('the women didn't get interviewed for a job'). All variables should be clearly conceptualised before they can be measured.

Poor operationalisation: Once conceptualised, variables should be operationalised in a way that matches this conceptualisation. Sometimes this is not the case. For example, if prejudice is conceptualised as a cognition ('women are useless') it should not be operationalised as a behaviour ('not giving a woman an interview'). Likewise, 'pain' may be conceptualised as 'the feeling of pain' but operationalised as 'request for medication'; these are not the same. Similarly, 'hunger' may be conceptualised as 'the feeling of hunger' but measured as food eaten. Given the complexity of hunger and why people eat, these may not be the same thing either. Observational measures are seen as more objective than self-report measures and so may be selected as the final measurement tool. But they may not match the concept being assessed. I remember reading a study that was interested in 'anger' conceptualised as 'feeling angry'. This was operationalised in terms of the amount of hot sauce a participant would put on someone else's food. These definitely are not the same! It is important to explore whether operationalisation matches conceptualisation, otherwise the measure isn't measuring what it is supposed to be measuring. The problem of poor operationalisation is illustrated in Worked Example 13.

Just a measure but not of the world 'out there': Researchers assess the usefulness of any measurement tool in terms of its reliability and validity. Good reliability and validity is used as an indicator that the measurement tool is really measuring what it is supposed to measure and is assessing something in the world out there (not just in the measure). But there are problems with the notions of reliability and validity which limit their usefulness. (i) **Reliability:** Internal reliability assesses whether each of the items in a tool measure the same things. This assumes that when a person scores a 4/5 on one item they should score a 4 (ish) on the other items. But should they? Healthy eating involves eating fruit but just because they eat grapes should they also eat pears, apples, oranges, and bananas. They might not like them all. For this, the measure would show poor internal reliability but if a measure shows high reliability it has just asked the same questions lots of times over. Further, testing and re-testing reliability shows that the measure is stable over time, but if we believe in participants who vary in time according to situation, time, mood, weather, etc., then why should any construct be stable? Finally, just because a measure has reliability doesn't actually mean it is measuring anything in the outside world. This is a fundamental problem with trying to measure anything and is discussed further in the final chapter on 'being

Worked Example 13 Poor operationalisation.

How to measure weight bias?

Background: Weight bias or weight stigma has been the focus of much research in the past 30 years.

Conceptualisation: It is described as negative attitudes and behaviours towards those who are overweight with studies showing prejudice, discrimination and stereotyping across social settings.

Operationalisation: Measured using scales such as Anti-fat Attitudes Questionnaire, Attitudes toward Obese Persons Scale, Beliefs about Obese Persons Scale, Fat Phobia and Weight Bias Internalization Scale (DePierre & Puhl, 2012).

Problems: These measures assess attitudes. BUT they also measure beliefs about the causes and consequences of obesity. These are not ALL components of weight bias.

Attitudes:	Beliefs about causes:	Beliefs about consequences:
Lazy	Overeating	Self conscious
Weak	Poor eating habits	Insecure
Untidy	Not enough exercise	Low self esteem
Less aggressive	Inactive	Feel unattractive
Sociable	**These are not weight**	Healthy
Self indulgent	**bias but beliefs about**	Dissatisfied with
These are	**causes which are**	themselves
weight bias	**backed up by**	**These are beliefs about**
	evidence	**consequences of obesity.**
		They may well be
		consequences of weight
		bias. But they are not bias.

extra critical'. (ii) **Validity:** Different tests of validity test one measure against other measures. A new questionnaire would be correlated against a more established measure, a clinical interview, or assessed to see whether it predicted a further measure of the same variable in the future. This is standard practice but its circularity is problematic. What if the established measure is wrong? What if both measures are wrong but equally wrong? What if both of them have nothing at all to do with anything in the world out there but are just a set of questions correlating with another set of questions. There remains a gap between what is on the questionnaire and what is in someone's head and just because different measures correlate doesn't mean they reflect what is in someone's head. This is also discussed in the final chapter and presents a fundamental problem to any discipline trying to study variables that cannot be seen.

SUBJECTIVITY AND BIAS

As with all parts of research, bias is also a problem for measurement and is a result of the subjectivity of both the responder and the researcher.

Responder bias: Many measures ask participants to self-report not only their demographic details (e.g. age, sex, marital status), but also their behaviour (e.g. smoking, exercise, diet, sexual habits), beliefs (e.g. attitudes to women), emotions (e.g. fear, embarrassment), or symptoms (e.g. tiredness, pain, hunger). Ideally, answers would be given in an open and honest way, which is why researchers emphasise the anonymity and confidentiality of the data. However, there are a number of conscious and unconscious reasons why responses may be biased and not as honest as desired. Some of these are illustrated in Worked Example 14.

Worked Example 14 The problem of responder bias.

Reported changes in symptoms following treatment for Chronic Fatigue Syndrome (CFS; Geraghty, Hann, & Kurtev, 2017).

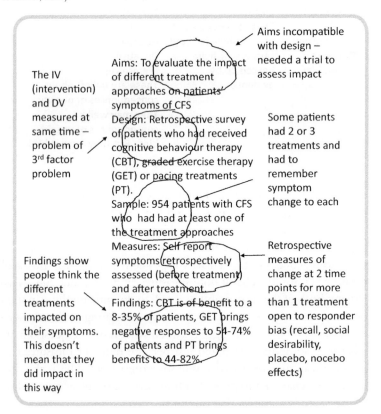

The IV (intervention) and DV measured at same time – problem of 3rd factor problem

Aims: To evaluate the impact of different treatment approaches on patients' symptoms of CFS

Aims incompatible with design – needed a trial to assess impact

Design: Retrospective survey of patients who had received cognitive behaviour therapy (CBT), graded exercise therapy (GET) or pacing treatments (PT).

Some patients had 2 or 3 treatments and had to remember symptom change to each

Sample: 954 patients with CFS who had had at least one of the treatment approaches

Measures: Self report symptoms retrospectively assessed (before treatment) and after treatment.

Findings show people think the different treatments impacted on their symptoms. This doesn't mean that they did impact in this way

Findings: CBT is of benefit to a 8-35% of patients, GET brings negative responses to 54-74% of patients and PT brings benefits to 44-82%.

Retrospective measures of change at 2 time points for more than 1 treatment open to responder bias (recall, social desirability, placebo, nocebo effects)

(i) **Recall:** The simplest form of responder bias is due to a problem with recall; patients may have forgotten what they are being asked to describe. Alternatively, they may remember but this memory has changed over time and bears little resemblance to how they originally felt. This is particularly a problem for retrospective measures. (ii) **Social desirability:** It is clear that responders often give socially desirable answers either to please the researcher or because they are embarrassed of what they actually do or think, or are fearful of the consequences if they tell the truth. Therefore, a researcher who stands outside a doctor's surgery to ask patients if they smoke might hear that very few say they do, as patients may want to give the 'right answer' to please the researcher, be ashamed of smoking, or fearful that their doctor will find out and treat them differently. People might be more likely to say they smoke to a researcher, who also smokes standing in a smoking area at a train station. (iii) **Placebo effects:** 'Placebo' means 'to please' and due to unconscious processes physical and mental symptoms can get better due to the participant unconsciously wanting them to get better to please someone else (the researcher, doctor, parents etc.). This is why trials often have a placebo arm to control for the unconscious changes due to this form of responder bias. Therefore, if a participant is in a study to explore the impact of a nicotine patch on the cigarette cravings, their cravings will improve even if the patch has no nicotine in it. Likewise, if a participant is trying out the impact of exercise on their headaches, the headaches may get better to please the researcher. (iv) **Nocebo effects:** There is also evidence unconscious changes can also make experiences get worse. This is the nocebo effect. For example, if a patient in a drug trial was warned that the drug may cause unpleasant side effects such as nausea or dizziness, they may well experience these symptoms even though they have been given the inert placebo drug. (v) **Privacy violation:** Some participants may not answer accurately for more conscious reasons and may feel that 'it is none of your business' and that 'you don't need to know'. More personal questions relating to age, sexual preference or behaviour, weight, income, or marital status may therefore generate false answers due to a sense of privacy violation. (vi) **Sabotage:** Most participants in research studies have consented and therefore take part in earnest. A minority, however, may wish to sabotage the study or may just get bored and not take it seriously. When this happens, answers can seem non-sensical (my gender: frog) or unlikely (all answers are '1' out of 5). These should be discarded, but more subtle forms of sabotage may not be detected and will influence the results.

Researcher bias: Researchers are also subjective beings and their subjectivity can lead to a form of bias in the measurement process:

(i) **Conceptualisation:** The way researchers feel about certain constructs can change the way that concept is conceptualised. For example, stress can be considered either a positive motivator that leads to achievement or a negative sense of being overwhelmed. The researcher's own views will influence how key variables are conceptualised. (ii) **Operationalisation:** The researcher's own views will also influence how a variable is operationalised and which measurement tool is selected. This is a particularly apparent across different disciplines. For example, biologists see hunger as a product of brain chemicals and gut hormones and measure it using these as their focus. In contrast, psychologists see hunger as a perception and so ask participants how they feel. The researcher's own views clearly influence what approach they take to measurement, which influences the findings. This level of bias is also apparent in more contentious areas of research such as the impact of termination or pregnancy (abortion). Researchers often have strong views about abortion and their research is clearly influenced by this. For example, those who are more pro-life and believe abortion is wrong and damaging will include 'negative' measures of factors such as depression, anxiety, and regret. In contrast, those in support of abortion will include more 'positive' measures of freedom, adjustment, self-esteem, and coping. This clearly influences whatever results are found.

. . . .

CONTAMINATION BY MEASUREMENT

It is becoming increasingly clear that measurement is not a passive process and that variables are changed by measuring them. This has been found for both self-report measures and the use of observation. (i) **The mere measurement effect:** When using self-report measures the aim is to find out what people think, feel, or do in their lives; not to change it. But research shows that simply asking people to complete a questionnaire can change the very variables being measured. For example, asking someone to rate their mood (do you feel sad/miserable/unhappy/guilt) can change their mood; asking them for their attitudes (do you think women are lazy/disorganised/demanding) can change their attitudes and even asking for their behaviour (do you practice safe sex?) can change what they do. This has been labelled the mere measurement effect and is not surprising given that we use this process to bring about change in other settings. For example, a mood induction task asks people to read a long list of negative mood states to induce negative mood and a food diary asks people to describe what they eat, to encourage self-monitoring and change what they eat. Words are powerful, so it is not surprising that the words in measures are also powerful. (ii) **The Hawthorn effect:** Observational measures are seen as less biased, as they don't involve the participant. It has been clear for decades, however, that observational methods are not a passive process and that this measurement approach also changes what is being measured. For example, if I sat in a restaurant to observe what people ate; sat in a hospital waiting room to observe how nurses managed their patients; or went to a school to observe a classroom, my presence would change the dynamics of the room which in turn would change how people behaved. This clearly happens when the researcher is obvious and participants need to give their consent. It also seems to happen in more subtle and covert participant observation studies. This isn't surprising either if we think about how we use observation and 'an other' to change things in other settings. For example, in couple counselling, being 'watched' by the counsellor changes how couples interact with each other; having legal support in an interview room changes the interaction between the police officer and offender and putting a camera in front of people changes everything. Contamination by measurement is illustrated in Worked Example 15.

Worked Example 15 Contamination by measurement.

Examples of the mere measurement effect.

Measurement	Impact
Do you feel sad, lonely, miserable and unhappy?	I now feel depressed
Do you intend to stop smoking?	Maybe I should give up smoking
Do you think female condoms are uncomfortable, difficult to use, embarrassing and ruin sex?	Female condoms sounds horrible
How many sexual partners have you ever had: 0-30; 31-60;61-100; 100-150; 150+	I am not very sexually experienced. Maybe I should have more partners
How much alcohol do you drink: 1-2 units per week; 2-4 units per week; 5-6 units per week; 7-8 units per week; 9-10 units per week; >10 units per week	I drink more than that. Maybe I should cut down.

REIFICATION

The final issue with the measurement process is the problem of reification meaning 'to make into a concrete thing'. Much research is focused on vague and ambiguous notions such as mood, beliefs, values, attitudes, feelings, or experiences and requires the stages of conceptualisation and operationalisation to enable the choice of an appropriate measurement tool. This means that these vague and ambiguous notions can be measured. It also means that we start to believe that they are no longer vague and ambiguous notions but concrete things. For example, depression is a complex mood state experienced differently by different people and changes across time and situation. It is vague. But once we have a depression measure (the GHQ, HAD, BDI) it becomes a 'thing' and the vagueness disappears. What these measures, measure, is no longer seen as a good attempt or an approximation of depression but depression itself. They measure depression and what depression is. Likewise, pain measures make pain seem 'a thing' and measures of beliefs make these beliefs seem 'concrete'. Reification is problematic because researchers stop questioning what they and others are measuring; they stop thinking critically about the theories that are built on these measures; and they stop wondering about the findings coming out of these measures. Reification means that the measures become all there is and the vagueness and ambiguity behind them is lost.

IN SUMMARY

Thinking critically about research means being aware of the many problems associated with the process of measurement. This involves questioning whether the measurement tool is actually measuring what it is supposed to be measuring; the problem of subjectivity and bias for both the responder and researcher; an awareness that measurement is not a passive process and can contaminate the very thing it is trying to measure; and a recognition of how the measurement process can lead to reification whereby our vague and ambiguous notions start to seem like concrete things.

9

THINKING CRITICALLY ABOUT DATA ANALYSIS

OVERVIEW

Quantitative methods involve the collection of numerical data that is then analysed using statistics. Qualitative methods collect non-numerical data that is analysed in terms of patterns in the form of categories, themes, or a narrative. Chapter 5 described the key components of qualitative and quantitative analysis. This chapter describes how to think critically about data analysis in terms of an awareness of the assumptions behind both quantitative and qualitative analysis and whether these two approaches are as different as sometimes assumed. In particular, it explores the issues of deductive and inductive approaches, the role of chance, the notion of a population, and the problem of generalisability.

THE ASSUMPTIONS BEHIND DATA ANALYSIS

WHAT ARE THE ASSUMPTIONS BEHIND QUANTITATIVE DATA ANALYSIS?

Each statistical test has its own assumptions about data which if violated invalidate the test. For example, parametric tests (e.g. t-tests, ANOVA, Pearson's correlation) should only be used on parametric data (not skewed) and if data is skewed then non-parametric tests should be used (e.g. Chi-square, Kruskal Wallis, Spearman's correlation). Sometimes these rules are not followed. Quantitative data analysis is also underpinned by three core assumptions:

Deductive not inductive: Most quantitative data analysis is deductive in that the researcher has an a priori question or hypothesis that they use to design the study and frame their data analysis. This sits within the hypothetico-deductive approach to research and is top-down rather than the inductive approach, which is bottom-up. Deductive research is guided by previous research, theory, and the identified gap in the research. Often in reality, however, research generates many variables and many possible stories and narratives. The creative process is there-fore to explore these possible stories and pull the data together which fits with existing research and theory in ways that may not have been thought of before. This is clearly an inductive rather than deductive process and quantitative research is often a combination of both deduc-tive and inductive approaches. This comes with the additional problem of chance, which is the fundamental assumption behind the p-value.

Chance: Many tests use the p-value to see if the findings are significant which explores whether any differences in the data are larger than they would be by chance and uses a random cut off point to decide whether a finding is significant or not (usually $p<0.05$ or $p<0.01$). This means that traditionally we have been happy to accept a 95% probability that there is a difference (or association) and a 5% probability that the differ-ence is just chance. If you explain this to someone outside of research, they might think that a 5% risk of a chance finding was actually quite high! P-values have dominated research for decades but the tide is now turning as there are many problems with this approach: (i) **Influenced by sample size:** The p-value is highly influenced by sample size so the larger the sample the smaller the p-value and the more likely it is that a difference will become significant (i.e. false positives and the type 1 error). Therefore, in a huge sample, a very small difference can come out as being significant. The p-value is therefore not an indication of the effect size (i.e. $p=0.0001$ is not a larger effect size than $p=0.05$) but just an indication of whether it falls into a randomly chosen level of significance; (ii) **A fishing exercise:** The p-value is open to 'data mining' or 'fishing' as the more tests you carry out the higher the chances are that one will be significant (i.e. 1 in 20); (iii) **A black and white approach:** The focus on p-values has resulted in a dichotomous approach to research to say the findings either are or aren't significant as opposed to asking 'how meaningful/different/associated are the variables'?; (iv) **The null hypothesis:** The p-value is actually not only based upon chance and a random cut off but also on the use of the null hypothesis. The null hypothesis (H_0) is the pre-diction that there will not be a difference between two groups. The alternative hypothesis (H_1) is that there will be a difference. The cut off for the p-values provides a criterion to decide whether the null hypothesis can be accepted or rejected. This is a bit like the legal posi-tion of being innocent until proven guilty. It seems a fairly twisted way of deciding whether or not there is or is not a difference; (v) **Dodgy practices:** The focus on p-values has therefore resulted in a number of 'dodgy' research practices such as collecting more data until the p-value is significant, fishing in a data set to find results that are significant, and rounding p-values down to make them significant. These have all been driven by journal editors' publication bias towards only publishing significant findings and researchers' desire to be published and have been called 'p hacking'.

The population: The CI and effect size is an improvement on the p-value as they no longer use chance to describe the findings but the wider population that we want to generalise to. Further, they aren't influenced by sample size in the same way as the p-value removing the risk of type 1 errors and this approach gives an effect size. I am new to this new way of analysis and I wonder the following: (i) **Can we still generalise?** If we do not sample properly, or tell the computer our response rates, or tell the computer who we want to generalise to how can it generate CIs that in any way reflect the wider population from our small and very biased data set? What it creates is a virtual population based upon the data we have given it. This virtual population is just a product of our biased sample yet we make assumptions that it in some way reflects the world out there; (ii) **What is a good enough sample?** When the computer generates CIs, a sample of any larger than about n=200 seems to make very little difference to the CIs indicating that the statistics believes that n=200 is good enough and approximates to the wider sample we are generalising to. If I want to generalise to the world (n=billions) or just Guildford (n=thousands) n=200 is tiny. So I wonder why the statistics seems to think that n=200 is was good enough? I also wonder whether researchers will simply continue to collect more and more data as they did before but just until their CIs no longer overlap; (iii) **A solution?:** To solve the problems of p-values and CIs statisticians call for power calculations to be carried out before data collection using the expected effect size to calculate the required sample size. This prevents research from having studies which are underpowered (i.e. too small and miss findings – the type 2 error or false negatives) or overpowered (i.e. so large that tiny effects become significant – the type 1 error or false positives). But if you haven't done the study before how do you really know the effect size you are expecting? (iv) **The same dichotomous language:** Finally, researchers using CIs and effects sizes still seem to use the same dichotomous language of research as before saying 'the groups are different', 'the intervention did work', 'the variables are related' – so we are still thinking like p-values even if we are pretending that we are not. In practice, researchers often report CIs, effects sizes, and p-values. They still say their findings are either significant or not and still use the dichotomous language as before but just cover themselves by reporting all sets of statistics. In addition, they use power calculations after data collection to justify their sample size or use them before the event (as instructed) but include spurious effects sizes based on previous unrelated studies.

93

WHAT ARE THE ASSUMPTIONS BEHIND QUALITATIVE ANALYSIS?

Qualitative data analysis is also predicated upon a number of assumptions: (i) **Narrative not truth:** There are a number of different epistemological positions within research which range from positivism (a search for truth and a belief that truth can be found) to relativism (the position that we can never know what is truly 'out there' as truth is constructed by us and the world we live in). Qualitative data analysis approaches vary in where they sit on this continuum with some using qualitative methods to access what people 'really think' and others arguing that this is 'just what they say they think'. In the main, however, qualitative data analysis is more concerned with narratives, stories, accounts, and experiences rather than the uncontaminated truth; (ii) **Inductive not deductive:** In essence, qualitative data is inductive which means that the data are allowed to speak for themselves and the researcher comes to their data with little idea of what they will find. This is in contrast to much quantitative research, which is often deductive and based upon the hypothetico-deductive approach which tests specific hypotheses. It is therefore not appropriate to use qualitative data to test a theory or hypothesis. It could be argued, however, that researchers have implicit (if not explicit) ideas that they are testing which is why they want to do the study in the first place; (iii) **Not based on number:** Qualitative analysis generates themes, codes, categories, or ideas and not numbers. The assumption within qualitative research, therefore, is that it is not based on number. When analysing qualitative data, however, a theme or category is more likely to emerge when it is more common and said by more than one participant. So whilst random idiosyncratic statements tend to be ignored, frequently occurring ones tend to be identified as important and coded as themes. It could be argued that number may not be explicit in qualitative analysis but it is implicit; (iv) **Cannot be generalised:** The final assumption about qualitative data is that it aims to provide rich in depth insights about the sample rather than ideas to be generalised to the wider population. Therefore, because of the sampling method (which isn't random or stratified) and the sample size (which is small), the data generated is not deemed generalisable and this is acceptable as the aim is not to generalise. In reality, however, no researcher or reader of research is only interested in the insights of seven people. They are looking for insights into people in general and so implicitly qualitative data is often generalised beyond the data because that is what motivates us to do and read research in the first place. Some researchers call this conceptual generalisation (in contrast to empirical generalisation) as qualitative research can generate new and exciting concepts (such as stigma) which are of relevance to all sorts of people everywhere. Some of the problems of qualitative analysis are illustrated in Worked Example 16.

Worked Example 16 The problem of narrative vs. truth.

Nourishing the spirit, drinking Ayahuasca, and recovery from Eating Disorders (ED), (Lafrance et al., 2017).

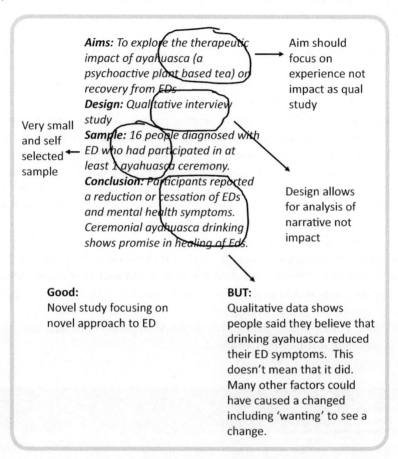

Aims: *To explore the therapeutic impact of ayahuasca (a psychoactive plant based tea) on recovery from EDs*

Aim should focus on experience not impact as qual study

Design: *Qualitative interview study*

Very small and self selected sample

Sample: *16 people diagnosed with ED who had participated in at least 1 ayahuasca ceremony.*

Conclusion: *Participants reported a reduction or cessation of EDs and mental health symptoms. Ceremonial ayahuasca drinking shows promise in healing of Eds.*

Design allows for analysis of narrative not impact

Good:
Novel study focusing on novel approach to ED

BUT:
Qualitative data shows people said they believe that drinking ayahuasca reduced their ED symptoms. This doesn't mean that it did. Many other factors could have caused a changed including 'wanting' to see a change.

HOW DIFFERENT (REALLY) ARE QUANTITATIVE AND QUALITATIVE DATA ANALYSIS?

Quantitative and qualitative approaches to data analysis are considered different in terms of their aims and the meaning of the findings they generate. But are they as different as often believed? (i) **Narrative not truth:** Many studies use qualitative approaches to explore participants' experiences (of illness, of treatment, of society, of school). These experiences, to some extent, are often used to describe what these situations (illness, treatment, society, school) are really like. Therefore, if a participant said 'I felt bullied at school' a 'narrative' interpretation of this would be that they 'say' they felt bullied whereas a 'truth' interpretation would be that they 'felt' bullied or even 'were' bullied. There

95

is often a tendency to slide away from the narrative approach and start to accept experiences as true. This is more in line with a quantitative approach. (ii) **Inductive vs. deductive:** Qualitative analysis involves a bottom–up exploratory approach to let the data speak for itself; yet researchers have pre-existing views that they bring to the research. Quantitative analysis involves a top-down approach with the researchers asking questions of the data; yet the data throws up surprising results and the researcher needs to find a story which involves induction and creativity. In fact, the question they choose to answer influences the statistics they choose to use which influences the findings they get. This process of choice is also a creative process. The dichotomy between inductive qualitative methods and deductive quantitative methods is probably less clear than is often presented; (iii) **The role of number:** Qualitative data generates themes whilst quantitative data involves numbers. Yet ideas are more likely to become themes if they are more common. Numbers are often implicit in themes. Again, they are not that different; (iv) **Generalisability:** Quantitative data comes from larger representative samples and can therefore be generalised to the wider population. In contrast, qualitative data comes from small unrepresentative samples and so isn't meant to be generalised. Yet most quantitative samples are not representative and shouldn't enable generalisability. And why would you only want to know about the minority of people in your qualitative study. Both methods lead to generalisations but probably should not. Perhaps qualitative and quantitative approaches to data analysis are not as different as sometimes assumed.

IN SUMMARY

Data analysis can be either quantitative or qualitative. Thinking critically about research involves being aware of the assumptions behind these approaches and the ways these assumptions can limit the interpretation of the findings. In particular, it is important to be aware of whether analysis is deductive or inductive, the assumptions behind the focus on chance, the notion of a virtual population, and whether or not the findings can be generalised beyond the data collected.

10

THINKING CRITICALLY ABOUT THEORY

●●

OVERVIEW

The final area for thinking critically about research is theory. Although theory often frames research and can be considered part of the basic structure to any research study, thinking critically about theory is more conceptually complex which is why I have left it to last in this section. This chapter will therefore explore how to think critically about theory in terms of two problems of meaningfulness and differences and two key tensions between the obvious and absurd and between specificity and inclusivity. This completes step 2 of thinking critically about research and the first question 'what evidence is there'?

●●

TWO PROBLEMS

Thinking critically about theory involves being aware of two problems: the problem of meaningfulness and the problem of difference.

●●

THE PROBLEM OF MEANINGFULNESS

When listening to a lecture, reading a research paper, or watching coverage of research in the media it is easy to sit back and accept it all as true because it is being presented by an 'expert' or published in print in an outlet that must be 'respectable'. But sometimes we get the sneaking feeling that 'this doesn't make sense' or might be 'just nonsense'. The first stage of thinking critically about theory involves trusting this feeling rather than pushing it away, thinking 'who am I' or 'I'm just being stupid' then working out exactly what the theory is saying and whether it is meaningful. It also helps to put the theory into simple terms and relate it to your own experience to see if it makes sense. This is illustrated by both past and current theories.

> **Past theories:** In the past, there have been many theories that were considered meaningful in their time but have now been rejected. For example, the study of phrenology argued that human characteristics such

as aggression, perfectionism, intelligence, or musicality were located in very specific areas of the brain and that these areas grew bigger when people excelled in them. Scientists used to study the shape of people's heads to find out what kinds of people they were by feelings for lumps and bumps around each specific area and the Nazis used this method in WWII to identify people of Jewish heritage. A majority of people also used to believe that the Earth was flat and that if you travelled to the edge you would fall off. Similarly, humoral theory was endorsed up until the 19th century, which argued that the body was made up of phlegm, black bile, yellow bile, and blood. If in balance, the person was healthy. But if they had too much of one humour they became ill; excess phlegm made people 'phlegmatic' or apathetic; excess black bile made people 'melancholic' or depressed; excess yellow bile made people 'choleric' or angry; and excess blood made people 'sanguine' or hopeful. In retrospect, it easy to criticise these theories and see them as 'nonsense' but at the time if people had only critically questioned 'how come I am more musical than my friend but don't have a bigger bump where I should have one'?, 'when I walk to the horizon why does it change and not get any nearer'? and 'why have I never seen these humors'? then maybe they would have been seen as meaningless and not believed at the time.

Current theories: It is not just the past; however, that has meaningless theories. When AIDS started to emerge in the US a key theory was that it was the result of recreational drug use in homosexual men rather than a contagious virus. In fact, some conspiracy theorists still believe this. But a bit of critical thinking to ask 'why have some people with AIDS never taken recreational drugs'?; 'why is AIDS also apparent in heterosexual people who don't take recreational drugs and have had blood transfusions'; or 'why are children born HIV positive'? would make it clear that it is contagious. Even more recently, researchers in my field still argue 'Obesity is caused by genetics' and cite the statistic '80% of body weight is genetically determined'. I struggle with this as I know evidence shows that when people migrate to a new country their body weight increases to match that country (i.e. their genes remain constant but their environment and behaviour changes). I also know research indicates that body weight runs in friendship groups (who share environment and behaviour but not genes), and I also know that when I am ill and eat less I lose weight and when I go on holiday and eat more I gain weight.

It is therefore good to question whether theories are meaningful. Sometimes they are. But sometimes when you put them into simple terms and relate them to your own experience they just don't make sense. This is a good step towards thinking critically about theory.

• •

THE PROBLEM OF DIFFERENCE

The world is a complex place and there are many variables to study and many ideas about how the world works. To make it clearer, researchers rely upon differences so they can classify this complex world into more manageable chunks. To do this they use conceptualisation and operationalisation to define and measure variables so that they are different than each other. These 'different' chunks underpin the many boxes we see in our theories that describe these 'different' chunks and then see how they fit together. The need for different chunks makes research easier and is an essential process of classification without which we would just have a blur or unclassified 'soup'. But this need for difference also raises the problem of difference and whether one box is really different than another. This can be seen for constructs, stages, statistics, and associations.

> **Different constructs:** Theories are based upon constructs that form the core to any discipline. For example, sociology draws upon social class, gender, and culture; psychology emphasises mood, cognition, and behaviour; and medicine is based upon health, disease, and life expectancy. Critically thinking about theory involves questioning whether some of these constructs are as different to each other as often proposed. I have been a psychologist for 30 years but I am still not convinced by the difference between a cognition and an emotion: Is the thought 'I am sad' an emotion or a cognition? Once any emotion has a label and can be thought about, does it become a cognition? Can we therefore ever describe an emotion? Some psychologists also differentiate between different types of personality such as 'empathising' (relating to emotions) and 'systematising' (making things ordered into lists). This is hypothesised to relate to autism and to be gender linked. But I am very emotion orientated (and very people friendly) but like to order things (including emotions: I am happy because of xxx; sad because of xxx; and frustrated because of xxx). I am both these personality types; are these two types of personality actually different? Constructs are put into boxes and treated as different to each other but does this difference makes sense? The difference between these constructs may be far more arbitrary and blurred than presented but research treats them as separate and discrete as this classification process makes research more straightforward. The problem of different constructs is illustrated in Worked Example 17.
>
> **Different stages:** Some theories also have stages whereby a temporal order is attached to the different constructs. For example, morality is seen to develop through six stages grouped into three levels: pre-conventional, conventional, and post-conventional morality. Similarly, the Stages of Change Theory describes how addictive behaviours involve six stages from

Worked Example 17 The problem of different constructs.

Evolutionary origins of bullying (Koh & Wong, 2015).

Aims are in
line with
methods

Aims: To explore differences
between bullies; victims;
bully/victims; bystanders on
mental health and social rank
Design: Cross sectional design
Sample: 135 adolescents
classified as bullies; victims;
bully/victims; bystanders
Conclusions: Bullies had more
positive mental health and
higher social rank. Youth
bullying is derived from
evolutionary development

Design limits
any conclusions
about causality

The problem of difference
Participants were assigned to one of
the four mutually exclusive groups on
the basis of their self reported data
on bullying or victim behaviour. This
artificially conceptualises these
groups as different and then treats
them as different then reifies this
difference by testing for difference.
Perhaps there is not such a difference
between these categories

The problem of theory
Conclusion about
evolutionary
development has not
been tested by the
design or analysis.

precontemplation to relapse (DiClemente & Prochaska, 1985; see Task 7) and Theories of Grief highlight five stages of denial, anger, bargaining, depression, and acceptance (Kübler-Ross, 1969). Even the Sun is described as having a life cycle as it passes through different stages. These stage theories consider change to be discontinuous with each stage being qualitatively different to the previous one. But are they actually different? Or do they just merge seamlessly into each other, but we impose stages artificially for simplicity. And do they always occur in the specified order? And how would we be able to show whether they are different stages or not? Like with constructs, these stages may be more blurred and not as discrete as they are often presented. This relates to the next problem of difference: statistics.

Difference statistics: Research questions involve exploring differences between constructs (mood vs. cognition) or stages (denial vs. anger). They also look for differences within these constructs whether by gender (male vs. female), age group (old vs. young), illness group (cancer vs. heart disease),

Task 7 The problem of difference: different stages (Prochaska & DiClemente, 1982).

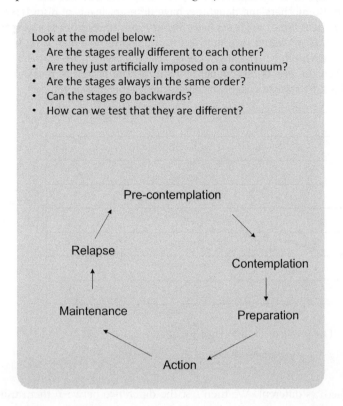

Look at the model below:
- Are the stages really different to each other?
- Are they just artificially imposed on a continuum?
- Are the stages always in the same order?
- Can the stages go backwards?
- How can we test that they are different?

Pre-contemplation

Relapse

Contemplation

Maintenance

Preparation

Action

or ethnic group (White vs. Black vs. Asian). These research questions are then tested using statistics which explore differences between counts (men vs. women) or means (mood vs. cognition). The results then tell us whether there is a difference. There are two problems inherent in this process. First, it assumes the groups, constructs, or stages are different in the first place. This may not be the case and the boundaries between these groups, constructs, or stages may have been artificially imposed. Second, by asking a differences question (men vs. women) and using a differences statistic (the mean for men vs. the mean for women) we inevitably find a difference (or don't) which **reifies** the notion that the different groups exist. For example, whether or not we find that men are stronger than women, by asking the question and testing the data with statistics the classification of gender into men and women has been reified. This **process of reification** can create **false dichotomies** whereby blurred variables become split into groups, constructs, or stages and through statistics, the different group (men vs. women), constructs (mood vs. cognition), or stages (anger vs. denial) start to seem real. The constructs therefore become different because we treat

This was a dyadic study exploring the disordered eating of mothers and daughters. If I asked 'Do mothers and daughters have different levels of disordered eating?' the answer was 'Yes. Daughters have higher levels of disordered eating than their mothers. BUT if I asked 'Are mothers and daughter levels of disordered eating related to each other?' the answer was 'Yes. The greater the mothers disordered eating then the greater the daughters eating. The choice of research question, determines the statistics used which determines the answer you get!

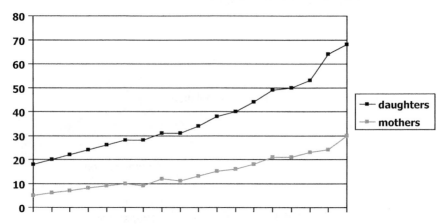

Figure 10 The problem of difference statistics.

Using statistics: What question you ask determines the answer you get.

them as different. We then test the difference between them using differ-ence statistics. The problem of difference statistics is illustrated in Figure 10.

The problem of association: When variables have been conceptualised and operationalised as being different to each other, theories then explore how they fit back together. For example, researchers might theorise that burnout at work is a product of coping, social support, and appraisal. These constructs are defined as discrete; the theory then hypothesises how they might be associated with each other. Likewise, researchers might argue that the recovery from a heart attack relates to the severity of the heart attack, changes in behaviour such as smoking and exercise, and a sense of control. These are defined as separate constructs that are then analysed to find associations between them. Sometimes the constructs are actually discrete from each other and it makes sense to see if they are related. This is known as 'truth by observation' or '**synthetic truth**'. For example, the theory that 'smoking causes lung cancer' is true by obser-vation and a synthetic truth because the definition and measurement of 'smoking' is different to the definition and measurement of 'cancer'. Many theories, however, involve 'truth by definition' and '**analytic truths**' which are more problematic. This is because they are **tautological** and associating like with like. For example, 'heart disease is caused by harden-ing of the arteries' is tautological and an analytic truth because 'heart disease' is defined as 'hardening of the arteries'. Likewise, 'depression' causes 'insomnia' is an analytic truth because the definition and measurement of depression includes a measure of insomnia. Similarly, the finding that 'how people make sense of their illness' is associated with 'coping' is problematic because the items used to measure both these constructs overlap. This problem of tautology is core to many theories and a product of imposing difference then looking for associations between these 'different' variables. It is not surprising that we find associations when we are simply compar-ing like with like. This problem of tautology is illustrated in Figure 11.

Are the constructs really different?

Many theories create different constructs and then see if they relate to each. If they are conceptually different this is an example of synthetic truths. Often the constructs are actually the same. Associating 'like with like' in this way illustrates the problem of analytic truth and the issue of tautology. The TPB (Azjen, 1985) can be criticised for this (Ogden, 2003).

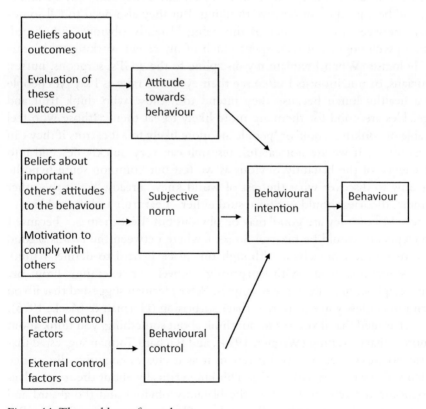

Figure 11 The problem of tautology.

Thinking critically about theory requires understanding whether or not a theory is meaningful. It also involves addressing the problem of difference in terms of whether constructs and stages are as different as sometimes proposed and whether this difference is being reified through statistics. Further, once constructs have been defined as different, theories often show how they relate to each and this can involve analytic truths and the problem of tautology.

• •

SOME KEY TENSIONS

Theories can also be critically analysed in terms of two key tensions: between the obvious and absurd and between specificity and inclusivity.

• •

BETWEEN THE OBVIOUS AND ABSURD

Theories should frame research, offer a new and interesting way of thinking, and be a product of creative thinking. But they also need to fall somewhere between the extremes of the being blatantly obvious and absurd. I am a psychologist but have spent much of my career working with non-psychologists. When I explain my discipline to these GPs, surgeons, nurses, dieticians, or nutritionists I often see their eyebrows raise as I say 'yes people eat a healthy lunch because they intend to'; 'those who think fruit and vegetables are good for them are more likely to eat them'; 'those who feel capable of cooking, cook' or 'people are more likely to eat carrots if they can access them'. If we are not careful, research can very quickly descend into the science of the blatantly obvious as we test our common sense hypotheses only to discover what the rest of world knew already. Yet at the other extreme, theories should not be absurd either. 'I eat fruit and vegetables . . . because I think they are good' may be obvious but 'I eat them . . . because I like elephants' would be bizarre! So somewhere between the two is a good place to position ourselves. Although this place is hard to define, I think it has something to do with 'surprising', 'novel', or 'exciting'. From my own discipline, here are some examples: Peter Herman suggested that if you intend to eat less you eat more – that's surprising (Herman & Mack, 1975); Wegner argued that if you try to not think about something, you think about it more – that's exciting (Wegner, 1994), and Richard Totman suggested that a placebo works better if you invest in it as it creates cognitive dissonance which was novel (Totman, 1987). Thinking critically about theory involves recognising the tension between the blatantly obvious and the absurd and working out where any given theory lies. There is a good test for this. Put the theory into simple terms, do the 'friends test' and watch for one of these three reactions: (i) If your friends say 'is that it?!' you have reinvented the blatantly obvious; (ii) Watch their eye brows and if they go up (in a good way) you have invented something surprising; (iii) If they laugh out loud you have invented the absurd. Be careful though as some 'absurd' theories can turn out to make more sense than we might initially think. For centuries, stomach ulcers were believed to be caused by stress. When Marshall and Warren suggested that they might be caused by bacteria this was laughed at as 'absurd' as 'bacteria can't live in the highly acidic stomach'. They turned out to be correct (by drinking the bacteria then treating themselves with antibiotics) and identified *helicobacter pylori* which has given us one of the most effective treatments of the past few decades.

● ●

BETWEEN SPECIFICITY AND INCLUSIVITY

Thinking critically about research also involves an analysis of the tension between specificity and inclusivity. There are many different theories (laws, models, and frameworks) used in research which range from the specific and focused to the inclusive, generic, and broad. Those that are specific can be clearly operationalised but only work within very limited domains and can always be criticised for what they miss. For example, Nudge Theory suggests that behaviours can be best changed by making small alterations to the environment and influencing the 'choice architecture'. An example would be placing fruit next to the till in a supermarket rather than being tucked away (this is illustrated in Figure 12). Similarly, the COM-B (Michie, van Stralen, & West, 2011; Michie, Atkins, & West, 2014) argues that behaviour is driven by capability (I can cook), opportunity (I have a cooker), and motivation (I want to cook). These specific theories are in part true, but are met by the cry 'but it's not as simple as this'. In contrast, inclusive theories miss nothing but are difficult to test and are seen as 'kitchen sink theories', a 'theory of everything', or a 'theory of quite a lot of things'. For example, the Behaviour Change Wheel (Michie et al., 2011) recognises not only the role of individual level factors but also 'biological and external factors' and 'includes environmental planning, legislation, and fiscal measures'. (This is illustrated in Figure 13). Likewise, Engel's Biopsychosocial theory (Engel, 1977) is a useful framework but is so inclusive it is impossible to test. Similarly, the Foresight report on obesity was so complex it was hard to use (Butland, 2007; see Figure 14). There is therefore a tension. Be specific and testable but miss something and make things seem more simple than they are or be inclusive and miss nothing but be unwieldy with limited utility.

The classic example of 'Nudge theory' are the plastic flies in urinals which 'improve aim'. This works for this very specific behaviour but is changing more complex behaviours such as diet, exercise, sleep, smoking etc as easy as this?

Figure 12 Being critical of theory.

The tension between specificity and inclusivity: being too specific.

Nudge: 'any aspect of the choice architecture that alters people's behaviour in a predictable way without forbidding any options or significantly changing their economic incentives' (Thaler & Sunstein, 2008).

There is tension between theories being too specific (when they miss out key variables) and too inclusive when they include everything. The Behaviour Change Wheel (Michie et al, 2011) can be criticised for being too inclusive (Ogden, 2016ab).

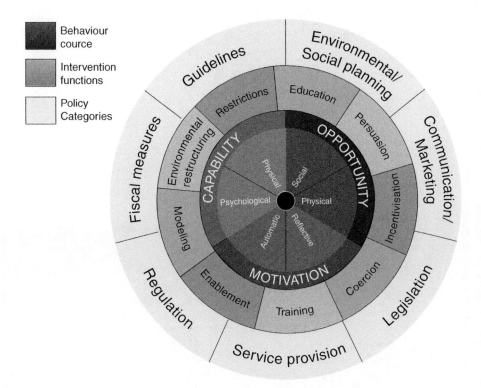

Figure 13 Being critical of theory.

The tension between specificity and inclusivity: being too inclusive (Michie et al., 2011).

The behaviour change wheel (Michie et al., 2011).

The Foresight Report on the problem of obesity was published in 2007. It was extremely comprehensive and included every level of every possible factor. It was impossible to implement in any useful way.

Full Generic Map

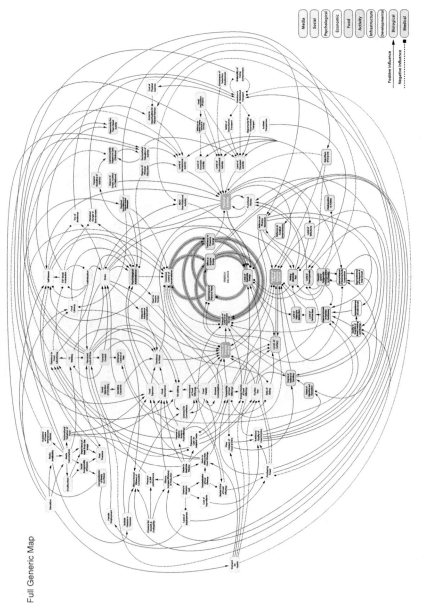

Figure 14 Being critical of theory.

The tension between specificity and inclusivity: being too inclusive (Foresight report on obesity, 2007).

IN SUMMARY

Thinking critically about research involves knowing how research is done and then being able to criticise each of the different components. This chapter has highlighted how to think critically about theory in terms of the problems of meaningfulness and difference and the tensions between being obvious and ridiculous and between specificity and inclusivity.

WHAT EVIDENCE IS THERE?

Step 1 involved knowing methods and developing an understanding of the processes involved in doing research. Step 2 then described how to think critically about each of these processes from the basics, through design, measurement, data analysis, and theory. This highlighted a wide range of potential problems with research that all limit the conclusions that can be made and raise questions as to whether any conclusions are justified. The next step is to understand the ways in which evidence is presented and how this can persuade the reader to believe what they hear or read.

THINKING CRITICALLY ABOUT PRESENTATION

HOW IS EVIDENCE PRESENTED?

11

HOW IS EVIDENCE PRESENTED? THE USE OF PERSUASIVE STRATEGIES

....

OVERVIEW

Thinking critically about research involves addressing the question 'what evidence is there'? and an awareness of all the potential problems outlined so far in this book. But it also involves asking 'How is the evidence being presented'? This chapter will describe a number of persuasive strategies used by academics, editors, journalists, and the media to persuade us that research is credible. In particular, it draws upon some of the ideas from the Social Studies of Science (SSS) and Discourse Analysis (DA) and addresses persuasive strategies such as being technical, using the social, and the role of language.

....

THE USE OF PERSUASIVE STRATEGIES

We are familiar with the idea that the advertising industry uses persuasive strategies to encourage us to buy their goods through words, colours, font size, 'experts' in white coats with clip boards, or 'celebrities' looking how we would like to look. It is therefore possible to deconstruct advertising messages to understand what strategies are being used and whether they work. From this perspective, the adverts are data and we can analyse them. Have a look at the image in Task 8 and think about what it is trying to say and how it achieves this. We are not so familiar with the idea that research papers are also trying to persuade us or that the media presentation of research might be using persuasive strategies to convince us of the truth of what they are saying. But if adverts can be read as data, so can research papers or media articles. This chapter draws upon the Social Studies of Science (SSS) and Discourse Analysis (DA) which although are very different perspectives with very different epistemological positions, offer a useful structure for analysing how evidence is presented and how we are being persuaded to believe it. Apologies are offered in advance to experts in either SSS or DA. This chapter does

Task 8 How is the evidence being presented?

not pretend to do justice to either of these complex approaches but to steal from them in a pragmatic and flexible way to show how they can be used to analyse research as data.

••

SOCIAL STUDIES OF SCIENCE (SSS)

Up until about 1960, science was seen as a straightforward investigation of the world and scientists carried out their work in a straightforward way. In the 1970s however, science itself became the focus of study. Researchers such as Bloor (1976), Young (1977), Woolgar (e.g. Lynch & Woolgar, 1988; Woolgar, 1988), Mulkay (1991), and Latour (Latour, 1987; Latour & Woolgar, 1986) turned their attention to the study of science and developed the Social Studies of Science focusing on the how scientific facts were constructed. This approach has involved detailed examinations of the range of methods used by scientists including: the networks of communication and social relationships between scientists; a study of laboratory culture and the mechanics of laboratory research; the role of company managers and the influence of the scientific community; the functioning of a physics department; the development of machinery and the research stations of radio astronomy. The day-to-day lives of scientists came under 'scientific scrutiny' to assess how their facts were created. This work produced detailed accounts of 'science in action' and classified and categorised the processes involved in the production of scientific facts. The researchers also coined the term 'a black box' to represent evidence which has become an accepted fact and therefore remains unchallenged and have argued that once a finding has been 'black boxed' it requires much effort on behalf of dissenting researchers to unbox it. These processes provide a useful framework for understanding how research is presented using persuasive strategies to make evidence become fact and ultimately turned into a black box. Accordingly, a research paper or a media report of a research paper can be read as data using the processes described by the Social Studies of Science. These processes can be classified as: being technical, using the social, and using language as follows:

> **Being technical:** From their analysis of the production of scientific facts, being technical emerged as a powerful persuasive strategy to make evidence seem more credible and ultimately 'black boxed'. This includes the use of large scientific equipment such as microscopes, MRI scanners, and mass spectrometers and well as the fundamentals of laboratory work such as white coats, test tubes, and scales. In fact, a study in 2008 by McCabe and Castel reported that papers which

included brain images rather than bar charts were rated as having higher scientific reasoning even though the reasoning was matched in all papers. Furthermore, the use of biological detail and the results of genetic analysis or blood testing can also be more persuasive as this use of the technical convinces the reader of the credibility of the research. Have a look at Tasks 9 and 10 and see how these images make you respond.

Using the social: SSS researchers described 'actor networks' to illustrate how scientists recruit their colleagues for support and argued that these networks are essential for building individual careers and turning one finding by one scientist into an accepted truth. This is part of using the social as a persuasive strategy, as research supported by many is considered more convincing than research done by a lone individual. Using the social to improve the credibility of research can also involve citing the work of others within a research paper (to show how the research is grounded in the work of others), having multiple authors of the study, or even having large anonymous research groups (to maximise the objectivity of the work) and citing experts stating 'Professor xxx argued that' or 'Researchers from the esteemed University of xxx found that xxx'. Even the use of peer review is a form of using the social as the paper is given credibility by apparently unbiased outsiders with no conflict of interest or agenda other than seeing that credible research is published. SSS researchers also describe 'science at a distance' to encapsulate the processes involved when one researcher's work is taken on by others in different research groups and different countries who publish independent research studies but

Task 9 How is evidence presented?

The use of the technical: brain images make evidence seem more believable (McCabe & Castel, 2008).

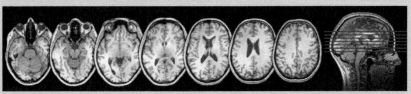

Using the technical through expensive and complex research machinery seems to be a powerful persuasive strategy and research shows that attaching images of brain scans to neuroscience research makes the research seem more credible. What reaction do you have to the images below?

Task 10 How is evidence presented?

Using the technical: using biology to give credibility to behavioural science.

Biology is also a powerful persuasive strategy as people seem to be convinced that a biological explanation is more convincing than an environmental and behavioural explanation. As a result the media can turn to genetics, blood tests and brain chemicals to make their argument more effective. Even in social science, articles on women's health (eg. contraception, birth experiences, women's health problems) are sometimes illustrated with biological images of the body. Below are some images of a large mass in a womb. What reaction do you have to these images? Do they feel 'scientific'?

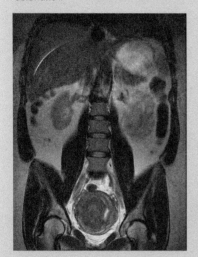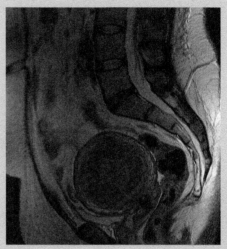

which add credibility to the original work. As seen in previous chapters, research is open to subjectivity and researcher bias. Using the social is persuasive as it objectifies the research and gives it the credibility of a body of reputable people beyond the subjectivity of those individuals who might be biased by the drive for personal reputation and distinction. Using the social as a persuasive strategy is illustrated in Worked Example 18.

Language: The third persuasive strategy identified by SSS is the use of language. From their analysis they highlighted the role of objective or technical language (equations, the passive voice) and the use and over-use of tables, figures, and numbers all of which function to mystify and jargonise the information they contain making it impenetrable to many and therefore more likely to be seen as 'science'. In addition, researchers may also draw upon arguments from the past to illustrate

Worked Example 18 How is evidence presented?

Using the social: calling upon other researchers to objectify research.

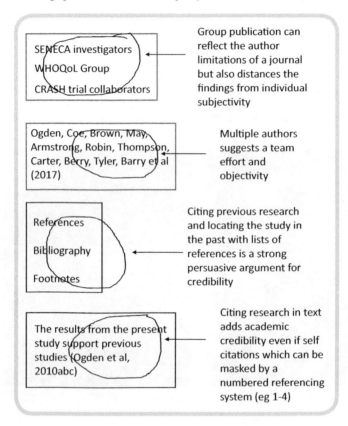

the constancy of their findings: saying 'it has always been the case' or 'researchers have known for years' can make an argument seem more persuasive. Findings which are variable across time and space can appear temporary and less credible whereas those findings which hold true across all cultures and all of history are more likely to be true. Have a look at Task 11 and see how this image makes you feel.

The SSS approach therefore explores how scientists create scientific facts and highlights a number of persuasive strategies which convince the reader of their credibility. If successful, these strategies will ultimately lead to the production of facts in 'black boxes' which will no longer be questioned. The role of these persuasive strategies, particularly language, is further illustrated by the use of Discourse Analysis.

Task 11 How is evidence presented?

Using language (an example of Structural Equation modeling).

One powerful persuasive technique is the use of technical language, jargon or numbers which mystify research. For some this can seem confusing but it can also make it seem more 'scientific' and credible. In contrast, simple research studies with simple take home messages can seem too obvious and less like 'proper' research. What is your reaction to the image below?

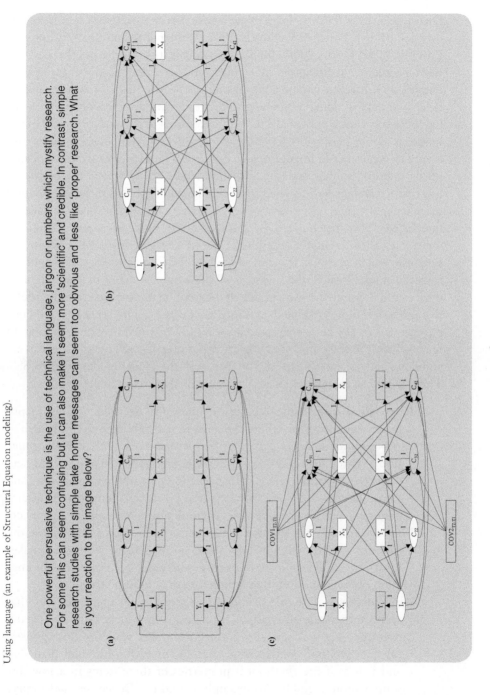

DISCOURSE ANALYSIS (DA)

Discourse analysis (DA) is a form of qualitative data analysis which focuses on the function of text (Potter & Wetherell, 1987; Wetherell & Potter, 1992; Potter & Edwards, 1992; Coyle, 2006). Unlike other qualitative approaches that describe what people say to uncover their beliefs and experiences, discourse analysis emphasises what text is doing. From this perspective, text (or words, images, behaviour etc.) is 'doing' something to the reader and for critically understanding 'how is evidence presented'? the text in research papers and associated media reports is 'doing' persuasion. Over the past few decades, Discourse Analysts have identified a number of linguistic devices that can be identified in text and analysed in terms of their function. This has led to the development of checklists that researchers have applied to a wide range of subjects including political speeches, pop songs, religious books, media articles, and naturally occurring interactions. Simultaneously, those involved in DA have also argued against the use of checklists stating that they make the process of analysis reductionist and simplistic which, they say, is against the ethos of the methodology. For thinking critically about research, this chapter will draw upon some of the key linguistic devices and illustrate the ways in which they can be used to persuade the reader that research is more credible than it might actually be. This is not to represent a pure process of DA but a pragmatic version of DA, which may be more akin to text analysis, but still emphasises what text is doing. These linguistic devices are as follows and several overlaps can be seen with the processes identified by SSS. These DA persuasive strategies are illustrated in Worked Example 19.

> **Rhetorical questions:** Rhetorical questions are those which do not expect an answer or where the answer can only be one thing such as *'Do you want to live in a world where our children die young'?* These function to bring the reader onto the same side as the text and start to persuade them that the text is going to be in line with their own views and values. Rhetorical questions are often positioned immediately after a comment but say the opposite to emphasise the comment just made. In research reports, rhetorical questions can be used to emphasise the findings and to highlight how these findings fit in with what makes most sense and would have been predicted. They make the findings seem obvious and intuitive – therefore they must be true.

> **Rule of three:** The rule of three is a repetitive persuasive strategy that seems to pervade all writing. It functions by adding emphasis to any point because there are always three examples, which is more powerful than just one. But its impact seems more fundamental than that and it is as if the rhythmical properties of three items in a row just sounds more credible. An example would be *'Doctors are hardworking,*

highly motivated, and committed to their patients'. This adds emphasis to the point but the power of rhythm is so strong it sometimes seems impossible not to use it. This book is full of rules of three!

Opinion as fact: One powerful rhetorical mechanism is to state opinion as fact such as '*Men are more aggressive than women*'. As researchers, we are trained out of this way of writing and use caveats such as 'research shows that', the 'literature suggests that', or 'from this it could be argued that'. But when trying to persuade it is more effective to be less evasive and more direct as this suggests that the weight of evidence is on your side even when it is not. However, when you have become skilled at thinking critically, such direct statements that state opinion as fact may backfire and make you wonder what is so wrong with the evidence that they need to try to persuade you.

Superlatives: Words ending in 'est' such as 'greatest' or 'weakest' or those prefixed with 'most' are superlatives and powerful persuasive strategies as they emphasise the importance of what is being said or the frequency of the problem being studied. For example, '*Autism is the* most *common problem in this school*' justifies why it should be taken seriously and emphasises how common it is. Likewise, saying '*It is important to focus on our greatest achievement*' also persuades the reader to believe in what is being said.

Eventualities: One useful persuasive strategy is to use phrases such as '*of course*', '*really*', '*clearly*', '*common sense*', and '*obviously we all know*', which have been termed eventualities. These terms make controversial statements seem naturalised and take away any controversy by appealing to a sense of normality and what everyone else thinks. Such phrases also block critical thinking by appealing to the reader's need to fit in with everyone else.

Emotional language: Using emotional language is also a powerful persuasive strategy. Therefore, rather than saying '*cancer has a high mortality rate*' it is more powerful to say '*cancer kills*'. Likewise, it is more persuasive to say '*men are more likely to kill themselves*' than they have a '*higher suicide rate*' or that '*obese people report self-hate*' rather than just '*low self-esteem*'. Emotional language engages the reader and engenders an emotional response making them more open to believe what is being said.

Pronouns: The simple use of pronouns such as 'we', 'I', and 'you' is also a useful persuasive strategy. For example, saying '*We all know someone who has had cancer*' draws the reader into the world of the writer. This brings them onto the writer's side making them feel less critical of what has been written. Interestingly, in academic writing, researchers are encouraged to write in the passive saying 'research shows', or 'it has been argued that' rather than 'I' or 'we'. This is also a persuasive

Worked Example 19 How is evidence presented?

The use of language as a persuasive strategy.

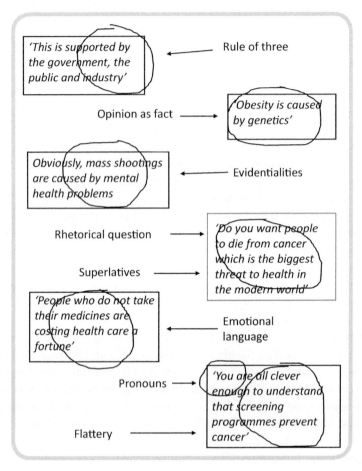

strategy as it makes the research seem less personal and more objective and therefore free from bias. It is unclear which approach is the most persuasive and it is likely that this depends upon the audience being persuaded and the source doing the persuading.

Flattery: A final persuasive strategy used to convince us that research is more credible is flattery. If someone prefaced their work with '*Psychologists are good at critical thinking*' as a psychologist I would nod in agreement and be prepared to believe what they said next. Similarly, if they said '*Nurses are extremely committed and hardworking*' nurses would then be more likely to agree with whatever else they had to say. Flattery builds the reader's self-esteem, brings them onto the same side at the messenger and then makes them more open to accept whatever comes next.

Research papers and reports of research in the media can be treated as data and analysed to assess the persuasive strategies used to convince us that the evidence is better than it probably is. DA is a qualitative approach that emphasises what text is doing and the function of text. This chapter has shown how a simplistic version of DA can form the basis to asking the question 'how is the evidence presented'.

IN SUMMARY

Thinking critically about research involves not only asking 'What evidence is there'?, but also 'How is the evidence presented'? This chapter has used SSS and DA to identify some useful persuasive strategies that can make research seem more credible. These can be applied to the original research papers with their opaque and conventional academic style and layout as well as to media reports of research with their more transparent attempts at persuasion. Both involve text, both are forms of data, and both can be 'read' to assess what they are doing to make us believe in what they say.

STEP 4

PULLING THIS ALL TOGETHER IN THE CRITICAL TOOL KIT

12

THE CRITICAL TOOL KIT AND THINKING CRITICALLY IN EVERYDAY LIFE

• •

OVERVIEW

Thinking critically about research involves the following steps: Step 1: Knowing methods; Step 2: Thinking critically about methods; Step 3: Thinking critically about how the evidence is presented. These steps have now been covered in detail to highlight a wide range of problems with research. These steps have also introduced the key terms that can be used to think critically about research and answer the questions: 'What evidence is there'? and 'How is the evidence presented'? This chapter will explore the final two components of thinking critically about research. The first is coherence and whether the conclusions are justified which can be assessed by using all the factors covered in this book so far. The second is the process of research synthesis and what happens when we combine different research studies. This chapter will then introduce the Critical Tool Kit in which I have pulled together the key terms used in this book. Finally, this chapter will look the role of critical thinking in everyday life in terms of dealing with facts, making logical decisions, and the role of uncertainty.

• •

COHERENCE

Coherence refers to whether a research study has internal validity, which in essence reflects whether the conclusions are justified given the theory, aims, methods, and analysis used. The extent to which any research study is coherent can be assessed in terms of the following:

(i) **Is the research question matched to the literature:** As part of the incremental nature of research, the research question should emerge from the existing literature and fill a gap; (ii) **Is the research question matched to the methods?** Research questions can only be answered with the correct research methodology. Therefore, the question should be matched to the sample and the design of the study; exploratory questions can be answered with a smaller sample and qualitative designs; causal questions need representative

Task 12 Matching the research components together: is this coherent?

Below are a list of research questions, methods and conclusions. Read each one and decide whether if this question was answered with this method and the authors made this conclusion would this be coherent?

Research question	Research design	Conclusion	Is this coherent?
How do people feel about exercise?	Experimental study	Exercise makes people feel good	NO/YES
Does exercise improve people's mood?	Qualitative study	Exercise makes people feel good	NO/YES
Do people who do more exercise feel happier	Cross sectional study	People who do more exercise are happier	NO/YES
Does doing more exercise make people's mood get better?	Longitudinal study	Doing more exercise improves mood	NO/YES
How does exercise make people feel?	Qualitative study	People say that exercise makes them feel better and gives them energy	NO/YES
Do people who are depressed do less exercise?	Cross sectional study	Depressed people exercise less than those who are not depressed	NO/YES
Does exercise make people less depressed?	Experimental study	Exercise reduces depression	NO/YES
How do depressed people feel about doing exercise?	Qualitative study	Depressed people don't feel that exercise will help them	NO/YES
Does depression change over time when you do exercise?	Longitudinal study	People's mood lifts as they do exercise	NO/YES
Is mood stable or variable?	Longitudinal study	Mood fluctuates hugely over time	NO/YES
Do men and women differ in their levels of depression and exercise?	Cross sectional study	Men do more exercise and get more depressed than women	NO/YES
Why don't women who are depressed want to do exercise?	Qualitative study	Depressed women don't feel that exercise is good for them	NO/YES
Does exercise reduce depression more in men than women?	Experimental study	Men's mood shows a greater improvement after exercise than women's	NO/YES

samples and an experimental design; process questions can be answered with cross-sectional designs. (iii) **Is the research question matched to the data analysis?** Questions not only need to be matched to the design but also to the data analysis. Therefore exploratory questions are usually answered with qualitative analysis, causal questions are usually answered with differences analysis, and process questions are usually answered with associations analysis (although in reality many different types of analyses can be used in most situations); (iv) **Are the conclusions justified?** If a paper is coherent in terms of matching as described earlier then the final question is whether the conclusions are justified and they should be justified if the paper is coherent. However, if the research question has been asked using the wrong design or the results analysed using the wrong approach to data analysis then the paper will not be coherent and the conclusions will not be justified. For example, if the research question is 'does exercise help with depression'? yet it has been answered with a qualitative study, then the conclusion 'exercise helps depression' is not justified as the wrong design and data analysis have been used. Likewise, if the question 'does overeating cause obesity' has been answered with a cross-sectional design then the conclusion 'overeating causes obesity' is not justified.

The notion of coherence is core to thinking critically about any research study and reflects whether the study has been carried out in line with its research question and aims using the appropriate design and correct process of data analysis. Now try Task 12 and test your understanding of coherence.

• •

RESEARCH SYNTHESIS: PUTTING RESEARCH TOGETHER

This book has mostly focused on thinking critically about an individual research study. Research, however, never happens in isolation and is always part of the wider literature. Each study therefore makes an incremental contribution to this literature and either supports or conflicts with research that has gone before or comes afterwards. Thinking critically about research involves an understanding of how new research is integrated into the existing research and deciding whether any single study makes a useful contribution to the broader literature. This involves the processes of rejection and support and ultimately research synthesis as follows:

• •

REJECTION

At times a new finding contrasts with what has gone before. This can result in the rejection of the previous research and can take a number of different forms.

Refutation: If one research study produces results opposed to the existing data this can refute the previous data indicating that it was flawed in some way and that the findings have been disproved. For example, the earlier findings may have been a product of chance due to the study being underpowered or overpowered The previous studies may have had weaker designs, have used the wrong design or have measured the key variables in an inappropriate way. Furthermore, the earlier work may have contained many of the problems with research identified throughout this book (bias, reverse causality, third factor problem, poor operationalisation, etc.). If the new study has a stronger design and fewer flaws than the earlier study, it can be said to refute the previous work.

Falsification: The traditional definition of a theory is that it can be tested and then accepted or falsified. Therefore, theory is said to have been falsified if new evidence emerges indicating that the theory does not predict what it is supposed to predict. For example, a theory may state that intentions to smoke predict actual smoking behaviour, but if research shows that intentions do not predict behaviour then this theory can be falsified. Likewise, if a theory predicts that objects fall when they are dropped due to gravity, yet an object is seen to rise, the theory of gravity has been falsified.

In reality: In reality, one study very rarely refutes all previous research as research is always incremental and all research has some level of flaw. Likewise, no theory is ever simply falsified by one study and theories persist even though research testing these theories indicates that they do not predict what they are supposed to predict. What tends to happen is that slowly, over time, the emerging body of work indicates that the earlier research findings cannot be upheld or that the theory cannot be supported. Then, after even more time, our beliefs about what we think is right change and research studies and theories are ultimately rejected.

SUPPORT

In contrast to the rejection of previous findings or theories, new research may reflect and support previous work. This then slowly, and over time, adds to a body of literature indicating that the findings are correct and that the theories can be accepted. This process can happen in a number of ways.

Replication: Occasionally researchers replicate previous work in an identical way using the same sample, methods, and measures. If a study's findings are replicated then this provides evidence that they were a strong illustration of whatever was being studied. The more they are replicated the stronger this evidence becomes. In psychology, there used to be a tradition of replicating findings and journals would publish the same study done several times in one journal paper. Due to the limitations of time and cost and the drive for new and different research papers, this tradition has pretty much disappeared. Nowadays, many disciplines are struggling with the replication crisis whereby it seems that many of our published findings are indeed a product of chance (or sometimes fraud!) and cannot be replicated.

Additive: In the main, researchers do not replicate previous findings but repeat them whilst changing the target sample or some of the variables. Therefore, what may have involved men in the past is now repeated on women, what may have used complex measures of quality of life involves a more simple measure, or what was used with patients with cancer now involves patients with heart disease. From this perspective, previous findings are supported and added to by extending their reach and showing that they also hold for different populations, in different situations, or using different measures.

Triangulation: An alternative approach to supporting previous research involves triangulation. This has been common in health services research for several years and often involves a mixed method or multi method approach to ask the same (ish) question but from different angles using different methods. For example, if a researcher wants to know the impact of surgery they could carry out a qualitative study with a small group of patients, a cross-sectional survey with a larger group, and a randomised control trial. This would answer a similar question but in different ways and would enable the findings from these different studies to be triangulated. This approach enables complex questions to be answered in different ways and recognises that there are different perspectives that need to be considered.

In reality: Although accumulative evidence that supports previous evidence helps to show that findings are correct, it is rare that any research finding or even any theory is accepted as 'truth'. In reality, most research findings come with caveats and most studies are flawed which means that research is always ongoing and very rarely is a research question completely finished and answered.

RESEARCH SYNTHESIS

Given the incremental nature of research there are now a number of formal approaches to synthesising research and exploring how each study fits together. These involve systematic reviews in which different research studies addressing a similar research question are evaluated and a conclusion drawn and meta-analyses in which the data from different studies are combined to create an overall effect size. Both these approaches involve a quality assessment of the different papers and sometimes follow the guidelines prepared by the Cochrane Collaboration or NICE which emphasise the problem of bias. These organisations argue that a quality assessment of research papers involves an evaluation of the internal validity and external validity of any study. Using their terms, internal validity reflects the extent to which the study's design, conduct, analysis, and presentation have minimised or avoided bias and external validity is the extent to which the results can be generalised to other settings. It is suggested that all research studies in any systematic review or meta-anallysis are rated for quality and that an overall quality score is created. There are different quality assessment tools for different research designs (qualitative, cross-sectional, cohort, experimental/trial). There are also more general tools that can be used across a number of designs. These can all be found on the Cochrane website (www.cochrane.org) or through NICE (www.nice.org.uk). Different research studies can also be evaluated and synthesised using very simple approaches such as a rating scale ranging from strong evidence, moderate evidence, and weak evidence, which enable synthesis across different methods and a simple take home message about the quality of research evidence. There is no perfect solution as complex approaches to synthesis lead to complex answers, which are difficult to implement and put into practice. In contrast, simple approaches miss the complexity of research but are more pragmatic. In the end, it comes down to a judgement concerning the quality of research (which is what this book is all about).

•••

THE CRITICAL TOOL KIT

This book has highlighted three steps to thinking critically about research and has outlined key problems and terms. I have pulled these together in the critical tool kit to facilitate thinking critically about research in terms of 'what evidence is there'? and 'how is the evidence presented'? The fourth step involves using this tool kit whenever you are reading a research study or the report of a research study in the media. The Critical Tool Kit is shown in Figure 15. Try using this tool kit against any research paper you have read or any media article describing research to test your understanding of the terms.

What evidence is there?	How is the evidence being presented?
• Researcher bias	• Being technical
• Representativeness	• Using the social
• Response bias	• Language
• Generalisability	• Rhetorical questions
• Reverse causality	• Rule of three
• 3rd factor problem	• Opinion as fact
• Ecological validity	• Superlatives
• Poor conceptualisation	• Evidentialities
• Poor operationalisation	• Emotional language
• Responder bias	• Pronouns
• Contamination by measurement	• Flattery
• Reification	
• Chance	
• The virtual population	
• Methodological assumptions	
• Coherence	
• Refutation	

Figure 15 The critical tool kit.

USING THE CRITICAL TOOL KIT IN EVERYDAY LIFE

The Critical Tool Kit is useful for assessing research papers and how they are reported in the media. But thinking critically is also a central part of daily life. We are constantly bombarded by information often presented as 'facts' that needs to be critically analysed. We also need to be able to think logically about contemporary problems and to weigh up the available evidence in order to come to a logical conclusion. These two components of our daily life will now be considered. This chapter will then highlight the problem of uncertainty and how this forms a core part of any research, any attempt at finding facts, and any attempt to think logically.

DEALING WITH FACTS

As part of being persuasive our friends and family, the media, as well as scientists present us with 'facts' as if they are beyond discussion and simply 'true'. Thinking critically about research can help with deciding whether these 'facts' should be accepted or whether we should be more skeptical of what we are being told. So far, this book has worked its way through research from the initial research question, to the chosen sample, design, measurement tools, and data analysis and then explored whether the conclusions drawn are justified. This is the order in which research is usually done, and if not, it is the order in which it is presented. When presented with 'facts' in our daily life, a useful critical approach is to do this process in reverse and ask 'If this fact were the conclusion from a research study what would need to be done in order to make this fact a justified conclusion'? In other words we need to ask 'how could we ever know this'? For example, if we read that 'drinking tea prevents cancer' then we need to think what sample, research design, measurement tools, and data analysis would enable this conclusion to be made. Then we would need to think if this is feasible and has it been done? Similarly, if we are told that 'Coffee gives you a heart attack'? then we can think through what kind of study would be necessary to make this a justified conclusion. When the question 'how could we ever know this'? is applied to any black and white statement of fact it quickly becomes apparent that most 'facts' are not facts at all: Either the necessary research hasn't been done to collect the evidence behind the fact or the necessary research is not feasible and never would be done. Have a look at the 'facts' presented in Task 13

Task 13 Are these facts?

'How could we ever know this'?

> **Below are some 'facts'. Have a look through them and decide if you think they are facts or not and what would we have to do to know this?**
>
> - Broccoli protects you from cancer
> - Statins prevent stroke
> - Men are more aggressive than women
> - HIV is caused by recreational drugs such as poppers
> - Autism is on the increase
> - ECT treats depression
> - Women are more body conscious than men
> - Social media is bad for you
> - Good weather makes you happier
> - Masturbation damages your eyesight
> - Lectures are a good way to teach
> - HIV is transmitted by sex
> - Mad people are more creative
> - Obesity is genetic
> - Wearing glasses makes your eyes worse
> - Exercise makes you live longer
> - Laughing is good for your health
> - Drinking tea prevents heart attacks

and think 'how could we ever know that'? in terms of what research would need to be done and if this is feasible. I have chosen this wide array of 'facts' as things we have once believed to be facts in the past, things that we didn't believe to be facts in the past, or things that we tend to believe are facts now.

THINKING LOGICALLY ABOUT LIFE PROBLEMS

Every day we make decisions about what to do, what to think, and what is right. This also involves a process of assessing the available evidence and coming to a logical conclusion. For example, if we are deciding what to wear we have to weigh up what the weather is likely to be like by considering the weather yesterday, the month we are in, by checking the weather app on our phone, and remembering what we last wore on a similar day that made us too hot, too cold, or just right. Then we get dressed. This all involves an assessment of evidence and drawing a logical conclusion. Likewise, if we are deciding what to vote in the next election we might read the manifestos (mostly not), reflect upon the past achievements or failures of the different parties, consider the recent public appearances of the party leaders, watch a debate or two then talk to our friends about what they are going to vote. Then we weigh up the evidence and vote. Similarly, when deciding whether to stay in a relationship we weigh up the pros and cons of the person themselves, our life with them or without them, and the ways in which our decision will impact on those we care about. Then we make a decision. In reality, many of our decisions are not based upon logic at all but on our habits, emotions, or values. So, we wear the clothes we always wear, vote for the party we feel most attached to, and stay or leave a partner depending upon our 'gut instinct'. But if we can learn to think critically about research, then we can also think critically about evidence in general and perhaps come to more logical conclusions about some of the more important decisions in our lives. Two of the biggest issues facing our world as I write this are the problem of mass shootings in the US and climate change. I have provided an analysis of each of these problems involving an assessment of the evidence in Worked Examples 20 and 21. If only the leaders of our world could be this logical.

DEALING WITH UNCERTAINTY

Thinking critically about research involves knowing methods and then evaluating what evidence there is and how it is being presented. This book has illustrated how this approach can be used to evaluate research papers and how they are presented. It can also be used to understand facts and thinking logically about life problems. Evidence, however, is hardly ever clear-cut. Studies

135

Worked Example 20 Using the critical tool kit in real life.

Some contemporary problems: mass shootings in the US.

Thinking critically is also essential to every day life and making sense of every day problems. Here is one example drawn from some core problems in the modern world which involve weighing up the evidence and drawing an evidenced based conclusion: the problem of mass shootings in the US, possible causes and evidence for these causes

Possible causes	What evidence is there?	
Mental health	High mental health in Japan, Australia, UK. No mass shootings.	☒
Men	Men in all other countries; lower levels of shootings	☒
Not enough guns	As gun ownership goes up, shootings go up	☒
Poor gun control	Mass shootings in UK and Australia. Increased gun control – no more mass shootings	

The problem
Mass shooting in the US

are mostly flawed (given all the problems outlined in the tool kit), the ideal study is often not feasible and cannot be done (for either financial, pragmatic or ethical reasons), and in our daily lives we are drawing upon all sorts of evidence beyond that which comes from formal research (we are scientists in our daily lives but our evidence is hardly ever actually 'scientific'). Furthermore, all findings, however good the study, only ever apply to some of the people for some of the time (due to sampling methods and the effects sizes found which are rarely absolute). We hardly ever find out anything that is true for all of the people all of the time. Thinking critically is therefore also about dealing with uncertainty and drawing the best conclusions given the available evidence. This still involves thinking critically but focusing on best-case evidence given the available evidence rather than rejecting evidence as either right or wrong.

Worked Example 21 Using the critical tool kit in real life.

Some contemporary problems: climate change.

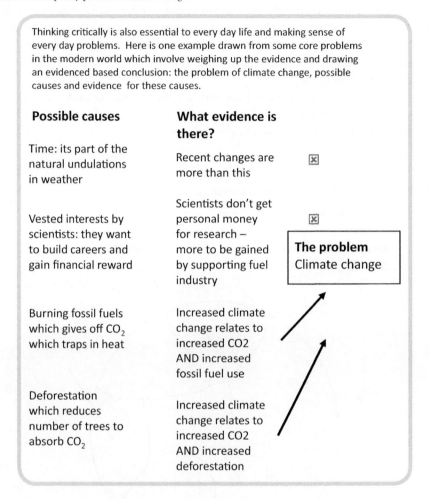

Thinking critically is also essential to every day life and making sense of every day problems. Here is one example drawn from some core problems in the modern world which involve weighing up the evidence and drawing an evidenced based conclusion: the problem of climate change, possible causes and evidence for these causes.

Possible causes	What evidence is there?	
Time: its part of the natural undulations in weather	Recent changes are more than this	☒
Vested interests by scientists: they want to build careers and gain financial reward	Scientists don't get personal money for research – more to be gained by supporting fuel industry	☒
Burning fossil fuels which gives off CO_2 which traps in heat	Increased climate change relates to increased CO2 AND increased fossil fuel use	
Deforestation which reduces number of trees to absorb CO_2	Increased climate change relates to increased CO2 AND increased deforestation	

The problem
Climate change

It also involves recognising that there is rarely a simple answer to any question and that no one factor is responsible for another. It is most likely that many factors have a role to play, but our job is to work out which factors are more important than others. One way to deal with uncertainty is to think about variance.

In research, we talk about variance in data and trying to predict this variance. For example, if we imagine that depression varies by 100%, research tries to explain as much of this variance as possible. Findings might show that of this 100%, 30% is predicted by gender (women get more depressed than men), 10% is predicted by social class, 10% is predicted by childhood experiences, and 8% is predicted by exercise. Our study may not be able to explain the remaining 42%. From this analysis we cannot be certain what causes depression, but we can see the relative impact of a number of variables. In addition, given that there is very little we can do about gender, social class, or childhood experiences, we may chose to focus on exercise even though it predicts the smallest amount of variance. We therefore accept the uncertainty in our model, but make an informed judgement as to the way forward. This is illustrated in Worked Example 22.

Now go back to Worked Examples 20 and 21 and consider where the degrees of certainty and uncertainty are and how to weigh up any available evidence to draw the best case conclusion.

Worked Example 22 Dealing with uncertainty.

The role of variance and the example of depression.

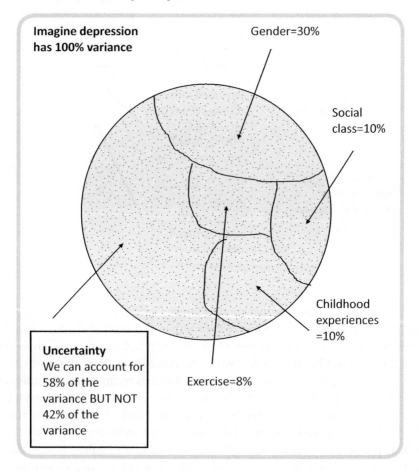

IN SUMMARY

Thinking critically about research involves knowing methods and thinking critically about what evidence there is and how it is presented. The fourth step in this process is using the Critical Tool Kit, which should hopefully be a useful resource for lecturers and students and could be used as part of a module. It could also be used by those who use research in their jobs including doctors, nurses, paramedics, occupational therapists, physiotherapists, counsellors, psychologists, teachers, or anyone who disseminates research to others (journalists, broadcasters, and even bloggers). Thinking critically is also central to everyday life in terms of dealing with facts and making logical decisions. The tool kit could also be helpful for these processes as we are increasingly bombarded by 'factual' information and need to draw conclusions for our daily lives. Finally, it is clear that no evidence is ever perfect and that thinking critically also involves recognising and dealing with uncertainty and making conclusions based upon the best-case evidence at any point in time.

STEP 5
BEING EXTRA CRITICAL

13

BEING EXTRA CRITICAL
TRUTH, DISCIPLINES, AND THINKING OUTSIDE OF THE BOX

••

OVERVIEW

So far, this book has outlined how to think critically about research in terms of the questions 'what evidence is there'? and 'how is it presented'? There is also a final step to critical thinking which involves being extra critical. This chapter outlines how to be extra critical in terms of questioning the notion of scientific truth, considering the nature of disciplines, and thinking outside of the box. This is the icing on the cake in terms of thinking critically about research.

••

QUESTIONING THE NOTION OF SCIENTIFIC TRUTH

Prior to the 17th century, knowledge came from the church and God was seen as the source of truth. Then along came the scientific revolution and through the pioneering work of scientists such as Galileo, Copernicus, Boyle, and Newton scientific principles were established. These principles introduced the concepts of experimentation and research and the endorsement of facts as independent of theory, accessible following careful and unprejudiced observation and a reliable foundation for scientific knowledge. From this new perspective, the emphasis was on 'observation', 'discovery', 'experimentation', and 'measurement'. Likewise, the epistemological position was of 'empiricism', 'inductivism', and 'positivism' and researchers set out to explain the world around them through the scientific method (Popper, 1959).

This scientific method dominated for the next three centuries and generated the research disciplines that we know today. In the 1960s, however, this perspective saw its first proper challenge in the form of Thomas Kuhn's book *The Structure of Scientific Revolutions* (Kuhn, 1962). Although complex, Kuhn's core ideas were as follows: scientists practice 'normal science' within a paradigm; a paradigm has its own rules of data, theory, method, truth testing, and validation; researchers are uncritical of the paradigm; when there are anomalies these are ignored; when there are too many anomalies that don't fit with the paradigm there is a crisis; this causes a scientific revolution and a new paradigm emerges. Central to this was his key argument that scientists are involved in 'puzzle solving' rather than problem solving. This meant that the answer to any scientific question was predetermined by the paradigm (as in a puzzle) and that the scientist's role was simply to find it.

These core ideas were problematic for the scientific method as they challenged the fundamental scientific principles. For example, whilst science was traditionally considered open to new ideas, rigorous with a search for truth at its core; Kuhn suggested that it was closed, repressive with limited paradigms that were simply puzzles to be solved. Further, whilst science was seen as incremental and evidence based; Kuhn's analysis suggested that it was static followed by paradigm shifts and a revolution. Finally, whilst the essence of science was that it was truth searching and emphasised change as progress, he argued that new paradigms were not better than previous ones, just different.

This challenge to the scientific method was unknown or ignored by many, but it was embraced by others and formed the basis of a new wave of thinking around knowledge in the form of 'relativism', 'social construction-ism', and the 'social studies of science'. These new approaches questioned the old order of the scientific principles and emphasised how facts were not discovered through methodology, but how methodology was the driver that created facts. Furthermore, research was no longer considered a passive and independent mechanism for the discovery of truth but an active and dependent process for generating truth. From this perspective, it became possible to ask 'how are scientific facts constructed'? The scientific method was no longer the method to be used in research but the object of research itself to be studied. My simple representation of this is shown in Figure 16.

• Science discovers facts

• Science creates facts

Figure 16 Being extra critical: the notion of truth.

So what are the implications of this challenge to the scientific method for thinking critically about research? This book has addressed the need for critical thinking to decide what to accept and what to reject and has used words such as 'fact', 'truth', and 'evidence' as differentiated from that which is 'wrong', 'a myth', or even 'a lie'. This final level of being extra critical questions this simplified dichotomy and suggests that the very notions of 'facts', 'truth', and 'evidence' should also be critically analysed. Therefore, rather than deciding what is 'truth' and what is a 'myth' being extra critical involves recognising either that everything is a bit of both, or perhaps (from a more extreme perspective) that there is no such thing as 'truth'.

CONSIDERING THE NATURE OF DISCIPLINES

Being extra critical also involves being aware of the core assumptions that underpin any discipline. These form the parameters of the paradigm within which the discipline sits and frame what questions can be asked, which research studies can be carried out, and what answers can be found. In Kuhn's terms, these are the shape of the puzzle pieces waiting to be solved. Recognising these assumptions means thinking critically about the very nature of a discipline. Some assumptions are as follows.

Things can be measured: Fundamental to most disciplines is the assumption that things can be measured and that what is captured by a measurement tool reflects the thing being measured. As described in Chapter 3 this process draws upon the theory of measurement and the processes of conceptualisation and operationalisation. Further, as described in Chapter 8 the measurement process is flawed due to issues of poor operationalisation and the ability of measurement to change what is being measured. But this process also involves a huge leap of faith that what is found using our measurement tools bears any relationship to what is actually 'out there'. Does a measure of depression really reflect what someone is feeling? Or is it just what was found on a scale? Does a measure of health status reflect someone's health status or just some numbers on a questionnaire? This leap of faith involves closing the gap between the measurement tool and what is 'out there' and although supposedly justified through techniques such as reliability and validity the gap is still there; we just have to decide whether to believe it can ever be closed. This assumption that things can be measured sets the parameters of any discipline within which members of that discipline function often without realising that these parameters have been set.

False dichotomies: All disciplines have constructs that are different to other constructs. For example, the cell is different to the organ, which is

145

different to the system; an emotion is different to a cognition; working class status is different to middle class status; a man is different to a woman; a child is different to an adult; and a patient is different to a doctor. As described in Chapter 10 this process of classification can lead to false dichotomies, which although useful for communication and simplicity can also create and reify differences that are not actually there. These false dichotomies, however, not only exist within disciplines but also between disciplines. For example, we dichotomise the individual versus the social and create the disciplines of psychology versus sociology; the mind is classified as different to the body and we create psychology versus biology; the organs of the body are classified as discrete, which creates the specialties of medicine: gastroenterology, respiratory medicine, dermatology, cardio vascular medicine, and neurology. Even the humanities show the same pattern with history, politics, and literature classified as discrete when they are all concerned with text, language, and narratives of both the past and the present. These false dichotomies function to reify the differences between disciplines which in turn establish the paradigms within which researchers from each discipline exist.

The hierarchy of disciplines: Due to this process of classification and the generation of dichotomies, we have a number of different discrete disciplines that use their own disciplinary approaches to answer their own research questions. From this perspective, these disciplines are different but not necessarily better or worse than each other. Sometimes, however, different disciplines attempt to answer the same question. For example, if we wanted to know why there has been an obesity epidemic, neuroscientists would point to reward systems in the brain; endocrinologists would point to gut hormones; geneticists would argue that it was due to genetics (or epigenetics); sociologists and public health doctors would emphasise the environment; anthropologists would argue for a role of culture; and psychologists would declare that it was down to beliefs and behaviour. Therefore, the dichotomies, which have generated different disciplines, have also generated different answers. Sometimes, however, these answers are no longer seen as equal but as existing in a hierarchy with some considered 'better' than others. In the current world, the more 'biological' answer seems to be considered more credible and accurate. For example, in Chapter 11 it was shown how simply presenting images of the brain can make a research article seem more believable. Likewise, a research answer which delivers information about cells, neurons, chemicals, or genes is often considered a better answer than one which describes culture, values, beliefs, or behaviour. This reductionist approach to science is very much a problem of the modern world. It wasn't always the case and probably won't be again in the future. But it means that not only have disciplines been created by false dichotomies, but that they have also been ranked by a false hierarchy. In turn, rather than simply being different explanatory frameworks with people choosing that which best suits their view of the world, this false hierarchy generates a sense that some explanations are better than others and closer to the truth. And we know the problems with truth!

Being extra critical therefore not only involves questioning the notion of scientific truth but also considering the assumptions inherent within any discipline such as that things can be measured, the establishment of false dichotomies within and between disciplines, and the belief in a false hierarchy across disciplines.

• •

THINKING OUTSIDE OF THE BOX

Once research has been critically analysed, conclusions have been assessed in the context of the methods used, and we are aware of all the flaws and limitations, we are then left with a finding. The final approach to being extra critical involves locating this finding in the bigger picture and thinking outside of the box. This involves asking the following questions:

Does it do harm? When doing research we are often enclosed within our discipline and driven by the goals generated by our disciplinary perspective. Then when these goals are met, we feel a sense of achievement and that the job has been done. All research, however, has the potential for doing harm and although any negative consequences may be unintended, it is useful to consider what the unintended consequences of any study might be. For example, in my discipline, researchers design studies to improve adherence to medication (Ogden, 2016c). Their goal is met when adherence is improved, but they don't always consider whether taking medication does any harm. They might improve adherence to taking statins, but statins come with side effects (the NNH – see Chapter 5). Similarly, researchers might carry out studies to encourage patients to attend for screening. The uptake of screening might improve, but attending for screening can lead to false positives and unnecessary interventions. Furthermore, researchers might identify vaping as a great way to promote smoking cessation and carry out a research study to encourage this new way of accessing nicotine. Current smokers may stop smoking cigarettes and turn to vaping instead which is better for their

147

health. But young people who haven't smoked before, may take up vaping, become addicted to nicotine and later turn into smokers (or just vape but would never have done so if vaping didn't exist). This is the unintended consequence. There are many different forms of harm which are not only physical (i.e. medication side effects, false positive, nicotine addiction, etc.), but also psychological (e.g. anxiety, depression, behaviour), cost (e.g. financial and time) and social (prejudice, blame, stigma, etc.). Whenever a research study produces a finding, it usually celebrates this finding. It is always useful to think outside of the box and consider any unintended consequences and whether this finding could actually do harm. The possibility for doing harm is shown in Worked Example 23.

Worked Example 23 Being extra critical: Does it do harm?

'Unintended consequences' seems to date back to the 19th century and the work of John Locke and Adam Smith. It was more recently popularised by Robert Merton in the 1960's. 'Do no harm', however, is part of the Hippocratic Oath and probably dates from the Hippocratic Corpus of the 4th or 5th century BC. Being extra critical involves asking 'does it do harm?'

FINDING		HARM?
Statins – prevent stroke	→	Cause muscle pain and diabetes?
Vaping stops smoking	→	Vaping encourages smoking initiation?
Cycle helmets prevent head injury	→	Deter young people from cycling?
Sun cream protects from sun damage	→	Causes vitamin D deficiency?
Eating fish is good for omega G	→	Fish contain mercury?
Encourage early help seeking for symptoms	→	Flood health service, create health anxiety and get false positives?

WHY DO WE ASK THE QUESTIONS WE ASK?

The final question to consider is why we ask the questions we ask and what do these questions tell us about our view of the world. Researchers ask many questions such as 'what causes cancer'?, 'why do people eat the wrong foods'?, 'can exercise reduce depression'?, 'what brain chemicals cause anger'?, or 'what education will be best for my child'? These questions may seem varied and cover the wide range of disciplinary perspectives but they all have two fundamental assumptions in common:

Causality: Underpinning most of our research questions is the search for causality whether it is framed as 'why', 'predicts', 'linked', 'reduce', or 'impact'. We therefore believe that events or actions are linked in a fundamental way and that one event (variable) has a causal effect on another event (variable).

Control: Further, the aim of most research studies is not only to identify causality but then to change one of the variables and bring about a change in the other variable. This reflects a fundamental belief in control and the ability of humans to make a difference to the world.

Both these assumptions illustrate a particular model of the world which although seems obvious to us now, has not always been the case and enables us to ask the questions we ask. First, this model frames the world as having **order** and as being predictable. Second, this model illustrates the assumption that people have **agency** and can impact upon the world. This model is starkly different to previous models of the world that were characterised by fate, chance, randomness, and passive human beings who were at the mercy of powers beyond their control whether they be Gods, the stars, or nature. Therefore, the final component of being extra critical is to recognise that we can only ask the questions we ask, due to a deep structure to our thinking that reflects a model of the world, very much localised in our current time and space and very different to past, and probably future, ways of thinking.

IN SUMMARY

Thinking critically about research involves asking 'what evidence is there'? and 'how is it presented'? Once this has been done, it is also possible to be extra critical. This chapter has outlined the final fifth stage of being extra critical in terms of questioning the notion of scientific truth, considering the nature of disciplines, and thinking outside of the box. This is the icing on the cake of thinking critically about research and is illustrated in Figure 17

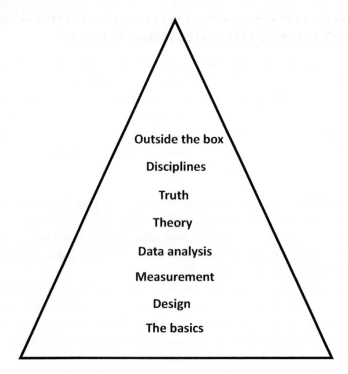

Figure 17 Being extra critical.

CONCLUDING REMARKS

For years I have told my students to be more critical. But for a while they didn't understand what this meant and I struggled to help them as it seemed vague and something to do with 'flair'. I then set up a final year module with a small group of students and started to realise what critical thinking was. And with the luxury of small numbers we had discussions (do dogs have arms?), debates (are emotions real or constructed?), critiqued papers (the male warrior hypothesis), pulled apart measures (what personality are you?), watched films ('an inconvenient truth'), and even played games drawing words such as 'epistemology' for the other team to guess. Slowly as the years went by, critical thinking became less vague and something that could actually be taught. Then a couple of years ago I took over a final year compulsory module with over 100 students in the room. No more drawing games, just clear lectures, lots of examples, a check list of ideas, and ultimately a Critical Tool Kit. So now, here is the book.

I hope it is useful for thinking critically about research for lecturers, students, health care professionals, teachers, journalists, bloggers, and anyone who uses research in their lives. I also hope it is useful as a life skill. We live in strange times and it would be good to think that armed with a critical tool kit, people in all walks of life would be able to make more logical decisions not only about their own lives, but about the ways in which their lives impact upon the lives of everyone else.

FURTHER READING

If you are interested in following up some of the ideas in this book here are some suggestions for further reading.

BOOKS

Best, J. (2008). *Stat-spotting: A field guide to identifying dubious data*. Berkeley and Los Angeles: University of California Press.
  This is a useful book for critically evaluating statistics.
Bonnet, A. (2008). *How to argue*. Harlow, UK: Pearson Education Ltd.
  This is a great little book that concisely goes through the skills of creating a coherent argument.
Chalmers, A. F. (1999). *What is this thing called science?* 3rd ed. Milton Keynes: Open University Press.
  This is a fantastic book that I have used a lot for my teaching over the years. It covers the limits of the scientific paradigm but does not show the reader how to be more critical.
Goldacre, B. (2008). *Bad science*. London: Fourth Estate.
Goldacre, B. (2012). *Bad pharma*. London: Fourth Estate.
Goldacre, B. (2014). *'I think you'll find it's a bit more complicated than that'*. London: Fourth Estate.
  Ben Goldacre's books give a great insight into the workings of science, journalism, and the pharmaceutical industry.
Latour, B. (1987). *Science in action*. Cambridge, MA: Harvard University Press.
  This is a wonderful book rich in ideas about how science functions.
Ogden, J. (2002). *Health and the construction of the individual*. London: Routledge.
  This is my attempt at doing a Social Studies of Science for social science. It reflects the time I got very excited about the notion of truth.
Woolgar, S. (1988). *Science: The very idea*. London and New York: Tavistock Publications.
  This is a really accessible little book about what science does and is.

PAPERS

These are some papers I have written doing a critical analysis on some of our theories in psychology. Read these if you are interested and as a way to show that in academia sometimes it is fine to think for yourself and have a go at things that other people see as truths!

Ogden, J. (1995). Changing the subject of health psychology. *Psychology and Health, 10*, 257–165

Ogden, J. (1995). Psychosocial theory and the creation of the risky self. *Social Science and Medicine*, *40*, 409–415.

Ogden, J. (1997). The rhetoric and reality of psychosocial theories: A challenge to biomedicine? *Journal of Health Psychology*, *2*, 21–29.

Ogden, J. (2003). Some problems with social cognition models: A pragmatic and conceptual analysis. *Health Psychology*, *22*, 424–442.

Ogden, J. (2015). Time to retire the TPB?: One of us will have to go! *Health Psychology Review*, *8*, 1–7. doi:10.1080/17437199.2014.898679.

Ogden, J. (2016). Celebrating variability and a call to end a systematising approach to research: The example of the Behaviour Change Taxonomy and the Behaviour Change Wheel. *Health Psychology Review*, *10*(3): 245–250. doi:10.1080/17437199.2016.1190291 (with five commentaries).

Ogden, J. (2016). Theories, timing and choice of audience: Some key tensions in health psychology and a response to commentaries on Ogden (2016). *Health Psychology Review*, *10*(3): 274–276. doi:10.1080/17437199.2016.1190295.

Ogden, J. (2016). Do no harm: Balancing the costs and benefits of patient outcomes in health psychology research and practice. *Journal of Health Psychology*. doi:10.1177/1359105316648760.

Over the last few years there are been many discussions about research issues such as publication bias, underpowered studies, whether studies can be replicated, and the need for triangulation. Below are some commentaries:

de Vries, Y. A., Roest, A. M., Franzen, M., Munafò, M. R., & Bastiaansen, J. A. (2016). Letter to the Editor: Moving science forward by increasing awareness of reporting and citation biases: A reply to Vrshek-Schallhorn et al. *Psychological Medicine*, *47*(1): 183–185. doi:10.1017/S003329171600218X.

Dumas-Mallet, E., Button, K. S., Boraud, T., Gonon, F., & Munafò, M. R. (2017). Low statistical power in biomedical science: A review of three human research domains. *Royal Society Open Science*, *4*(2): 160254.

Higginson, A. D., & Munafò, M. R. (2016). Current incentives for scientists lead to underpowered studies with erroneous conclusions. *PLoS Biology*, *14*(11). doi:10.1371/journal.pbio.2000995.

Munafò, M. R. (2016). Open science and research reproducibility. *Ecancermedicalscience*, *7*(10), ed56. doi:10.3332/ecancer.2016.ed56.

Munafò, M. R. (2017). Promoting reproducibility in addiction research. *Addiction*, *112*(9): 1519–1520. doi:10.1111/add.13853.

Munafò, M. R., & Davey Smith, G. (2018). Repeating experiments is not enough. *Nature*, *553*(7689), 399–401.

Munafò, M. R., & Davey Smith, G. (2018). Robust research needs many lines of evidence. *Nature*, *553*(7689), 399–401.

Munafò, M. R., & Neill, J. (2016). Null is beautiful: On the importance of publishing null results. *Journal of Psychopharmacology*, *30*(7), 585. doi:10.1177/0269881116638813.

Poldrack, R. A., Baker, C. I., Durnez, J., Gorgolewski, K. J., Matthews, P. M., Munafò, M. R., . . . Yarkoni, T. (2017). Scanning the horizon: Towards transparent and reproducible neuroimaging research. *Nature Reviews Neuroscience*, *18*(2): 115–126. doi:10.1038/nrn.2016.167.

REFERENCES

Aaronson, N. K., Ahmedzai, S., Bergman, B., Bullinger, M., Cull, A., . . . de Haes, J. C. (1993). The European Organisation for Research and Treatment of Cancer QLQ-C30: A quality of life instrument for use in international clinical trials in oncology. *Journal for the National Cancer Institute, 85,* 365–376.

Ajzen, I. (1985). From intention to actions: A theory of planned behavior. In J. Kuhl & J. Beckman (Eds.), *Action-control: From cognition to behavior* (pp. 11–39). Heidelberg: Springer.

Andrews, A. M., Zhang, N., Magee, J. C., Chapman, R., Langford, A. T., & Resnicow, K. (2012). Increasing donor designation through black churches: Results of a randomized trial. *Progress in Transplantation, 22*(2), 161–167. doi:10.7182/pit2012281.

Angermeyer, M. C., & Matschinger, H. (2003). The stigma of mental illness: Effects of labelling on public attitudes towards people with mental disorder. *Acta Psychiatrica Scandinavica, 108*(4): 304–309.

Bell, B., Jaitman, L., & Machin, S. (2014). Crime deterrence: Evidence from the London 20122 riots. *The Economic Journal, 124,* 480–506.

Björk, B. C., Annikki, R., & Lauri, M. *Global annual volume of peer reviewed scholarly articles and the share available via different open access options.* Retrieved from http://citeseerx.ist.psu.edu/viewdoc/summary?doi=10.1.1.162.991

Blalock, H. M. (1982). *Conceptualisation and measurement in the social sciences.* Beverley Hills, CA: Sage.

Bloor, D. (1976). *Knowledge and social imagery.* London: Routledge & Kegan Paul.

Bryman, A. (1989). *Research methods and organisation studies.* London: Routledge.

Burkert, N. T., Muckenhuber, J., Großschädl, F., Rásky, E., & Freidl, W. (2014). Nutrition and health – The association between eating behavior and various health parameters: A matched sample study. *PLoS ONE, 9*(2), e88278. doi:10.1371/journal.pone.0088278.

Butland, R. (2007). *The Foresight report.* Retrieved from www.gov.uk/government/publications/reducing-obesity-future-choices

Coyle, A. (2006). Discourse analysis. In G. M. Breakwell, C. Fife-Schaw, S. Hammond, & J. A. Smith (Eds.), *Research methods in psychology* (3rd ed., pp. 366–387). London: Sage.

DiClemente, C. C., & Prochaska, J. O. (1985). Processes and stages of change: Coping and competence in smoking behavior change. In F. Shiffman & T. A. Wills (Eds.), *Coping and substance abuse* (pp. 319–343). New York, NY: Academic Press.

Doll, R., & Hill, A. B. (1950). Smoking and carcinoma of the lung: Preliminary report. *British Medical Journal, 2*(4682), 739–748. doi:10.1136/bmj.2.4682.739.

Doll, R., & Hill, A. B. (1956). Lung cancer and other causes of death in relation to smoking: A second report on the mortality of British doctors. *British Medical Journal, 2*(5001), 1071–1081. doi:10.1136/bmj.2.5001.1071.

Engel, G. L. (1977). The need for a new medical model: A challenge for biomedicine. *Science*, *196*, 129–135.

Field, A. (2018). *Discovering statistics using IBM SPSS*. London: Sage.

Geraghty, K., Hann, M., & Kurtev, S. (2017). Myalgic encephalomyelitis/chronic fatigue syndrome patients' reports of symptom changes following cognitive behavioural therapy, graded exercise therapy and pacing treatments: Analysis of a primary survey compared with secondary surveys. *Journal of Health Psychology*, 1–16.

Harvey, S. B., Øverland, S., Hatch, S. L., Wessely, S., Mykletun, A., & Hotopf, M. (2018). Exercise and the prevention of depression: Results of the HUNT cohort study. *American Journal of Psychiatry*, *175*(1), 28–36. doi:10.1176/appi.ajp.2017.16111223.

Healey, M. D., & Ellis, B. J. (2007). Birth order, conscientiousness and openness to experiences: Tests of the family niche model of personality using a within family methodology. *Evolution and Human Behaviour*, *28*, 55–59.

Herman, P., & Mack, D. (1975). Restrained and unrestrained eating. *Journal of Personality*, *43*, 646–660.

Jinha, A. (2010). Article 50 million: An estimate of the number of scholarly articles in existence. *Learned Publishing*, *23*(3), 258–263. doi:10.1087/20100308.

Koh, J. B., & Wong, J. S. (2015, July 9). Survival of the fittest and the sexiest: Evolutionary origins of adolescent bullying. *Journal of Interpersonal Violence*, *30*, 1–23. doi:10.1177/0886260515593546.

Kübler-Ross, E. (1969). *On death and dying*. London: Routledge.

Kuhn, T. (1962). *The structure of scientific revolutions*. Chicago, IL: Chicago University Press.

Lafrance, A., Loizaga-Velder, A., Fletcher, J., Renelli. M., Files, N., & Tupper, K. W. (2017). Nourishing the spirit: Exploratory research on Ayahuasca experiences along the continuum of recovery from eating disorders. *Journal of Psychoactive Drugs*, *49*(5), 427–435. doi:10.1080/02791072.2017.1361559.

Latour, B. (1987). Chapter: Opening Pandora's box. In *Science in Action*. Cambridge, MA: Harvard University Press.

Latour, B., & Woolgar, S. (1986). *Laboratory life: The construction of scientific facts* (2nd ed.). Princeton, NJ: Princeton University Press.

Lynch, M., & Woolgar, S. (1988). Introduction: Sociological orientations to representational practice in science. In M. Lynch & S. Woolgar (Eds.), *Representation in scientific practice*. Cambridge: Kluwer Academic Publishers.

Macintyre, S., Hunt, K., & Sweeting, H. (1996). Gender differences in health: Are things really as simple as they seem? *Social Science & Medicine*, *42*(4), 617–624.

McCabe, D. P., & Castel, A. D. (2008). Seeing is believing: The effect of brain images on judgments of scientific reasoning. *Cognition*, *107*(1), 343–352.

Michie, S., Atkins, L., & West, R. (2014). *The behaviour change wheel: A guide to designing interventions* (1st ed.). London: Silverback.

Michie, S., van Stralen, M. M., & West, R. (2011). The behaviour change wheel: A new method for characterising and designing behaviour change interventions. *Implementation Science*, *6*(1), 42.

Mulkay, M. (1991). *Sociology of science: A sociological pilgrimage*. Milton Keynes: Open University Press.

National Science Board. Retrieved from https://www.nsf.gov/statistics/2018/nsb20181/report/sections/overview/research-publications

Nissen, S. E. (2010). The rise and fall of rosiglitazone. *European Heart Journal*, *31*(7), 773–776. doi:10.1093/eurheartj/ehq016.

Ogden, J. (2003). Some problems with social cognition models: A pragmatic and conceptual analysis. *Health Psychology*, *22*, 424–442.

Ogden, J. (2015). Time to retire the TPB?: One of us will have to go! *Health Psychology Review*, *8*, 1–7. doi:10.1080/17437199.2014.898679

Ogden, J. (2016a). Celebrating variability and a call to end a systematising approach to research: The example of the behaviour change taxonomy and the behaviour change wheel. *Health Psychology Review*, *10*(3), 245–250. doi:10.1080/17437199.2016.1190291 (with five commentaries).

Ogden, J. (2016b, September). Theories, timing and choice of audience: Some key tensions in health psychology and a response to commentaries on Ogden (2016). *Health Psychology Review*, *10*(3), 274–276. doi:10.1080/17437199.2016.1190295.

Ogden, J. (2016c). Do no harm: Balancing the costs and benefits of patient outcomes in health psychology research and practice. *Journal of Health Psychology*. doi:10.1177/1359105316648760.

ONS. (2017). *Internet users in the UK*. Retrieved from https://www.ons.gov.uk/businessindustryandtrade/itandinternetindustry/bulletins/internetusers/2017

Popper, K. R. (1959). *The logic of scientific discovery*. New York, NY: Basic Books.

Potter, J., & Edwards, D. (1992). *Discursive psychology*. London: Sage.

Potter, J., & Wetherell, M. (1987). *Discourse and social psychology: Beyond attitudes and behaviour*. London: Sage.

Prochaska, J. O., & DiClemente, C. C. (1982). Transtheoretical therapy: Toward a more integrative model of change. *Psychotherapy: Theory Research and Practice*, *19*, 276–288.

Roberts, I., Shakur, H., Coats, T., Hunt, B., Balogun, E., Barnetson, L., . . . Guerriero, C. (2013). The CRASH-2 trial: A randomised controlled trial and economic evaluation of the effects of tranexamic acid on death, vascular occlusive events and transfusion requirement in bleeding trauma patients. *Health Technology Assessment*, *17*(10), 1–79. doi:10.3310/hta17100.

Roberts, I., Yates, D., Sandercock, P., Farrell, B., Wasserberg, J., Lomas, G., . . . CRASH trial collaborators. (2004). Effect of intravenous corticosteroids on death within 14 days in 10008 adults with clinically significant head injury (MRC CRASH trial): Randomised placebo-controlled trial. *Lancet*, *364*(9442), 1321–1328.

Stewart, A. L., & Ware, J. E. (Eds.) (1992). *Measuring functioning and well being: The medical outcomes study approach*. Durham, NC: Duke University Press.

Thaler, R., & Sunstein, C. (2008). *Nudge*. London: Penguin Books.

Tollow, P., & Ogden, J. (2017). The importance of relationships in treatment for chronic leg ulceration. *Journal of Health Psychology*, *23*(8), 1075–1084. doi:10.1177/1359105317705984.

Totman, R. G. (1987). *The social causes of illness*. London: Souvenir Press.

Walburn, J., Vedhara, K., Hankins, M., Rixon, L., & Weinman, J. (2009). Psychological stress and wound healing in humans: A systematic review and meta-analysis. *Journal of Psychosomatic Research*, *67*(3), 253–271. doi:10.1016/j.jpsychores.2009.04.002.

Wegner, D. M. (1994). Ironic processes of mental control. *Psychological Review*, *101*, 34–52.

Wetherell, M., & Potter, J. (1992). *Mapping the language of racism: Discourse and the legitimation of exploitation*. Hassocks, Sussex: Harvester, Wheatsheaf

WHOQOL Group. (1993). *Measuring quality of Life: The development of a world health organisation Quality of Life instrument (WHOQOL)*. Geneva: WHO.

Woolgar, S. (1988). *Science: The very idea*. London: Ellis Horwood Ltd; Chichester: Tavistock Publications.

Young, R. (1977). Science is social relations. *Radical Science Journal*, *5*, 65–131.

INDEX